Life of a Lifetime

Also by Christoph Spiessens

Connecting to Your Inner Light:
Your Guide to Feeling Lighter and Following the Dreams of Your Soul

Life of a Lifetime

Inspiration for Creating Your Extraordinary Life

Christoph Spiessens

BUSINESS EXPERT PRESS

Life of a Lifetime: Inspiration for Creating Your Extraordinary Life
Copyright © Business Expert Press, LLC, 2017.

First published in 2017 by
Business Expert Press, LLC
222 East 46th Street, New York, NY 10017
www.businessexpertpress.com

ISBN-13: 978-1-63157-718-5 (paperback)
ISBN-13: 978-1-63157-719-2 (e-book)

Business Expert Press Human Resource Management and Organizational Behavior Collection

Collection ISSN: 1946-5637 (print)
Collection ISSN: 1946-5645 (electronic)

Cover and interior design by S4Carlisle Publishing Services Private Ltd., Chennai, India

First edition: 2017

10 9 8 7 6 5 4 3 2 1

Printed in the United States of America.

I dedicate this book to all readers who are committed to turning their ordinary life into their extraordinary life

Abstract

What if you could stop living your ordinary life and start living your extraordinary life?

You are about to discover the awe-inspiring reasons why things are the way they are in your life and how you can make them what you want them to be—for good! Here are the insights, guidance, and tools to show you how to bring out the best in you and your life.

A refreshing change from the vague rhetoric and over-complicated how-to's of the usual spiritual self-help book, *Life of a Lifetime*, makes complex mind–body–spirit concepts easy to understand and apply in your everyday life. It's all about simple, practical ways to empower you to make changes and create your life of a lifetime.

- Find out how to create everyday happiness.
- Learn how to eliminate the turmoil in your life.
- Discover your life purpose and what to do about it.

Keywords

Inspiration, Mind–Body–Spirit, Mindfulness, Motivation, New Age, Personal Development, Personal Effectiveness, Psychology, Self-Management, Spirituality

Contents

There are more stars in the universe than grains of sand on all the beaches on Earth combined. There are just as many reasons never to give up on your dreams.

—Christoph Spiessens

Introduction

In this book, you'll find something that's rare these days —simplicity. In an increasingly stressful world where good is never good enough, fast is never fast enough, and the bar is forever raised, simplicity tends to make people a little suspicious. Yet I believe it is the key to successfully navigating the difficult waters of today's demanding world. It helps create balance, change, and happiness.

The power of simplicity never ceases to amaze me. Time and again, I witness how it helps my coaching clients, seminar guests, and workshop participants improve the quality of their lives in a big way. Simplicity dissolves their often complicated concerns, fears, and challenges. And then they find it easier to discover their inner power, the solutions to their problems, and their long-held beliefs that no longer serve them. They can now make space for the fresh perspectives that will set them free.

I believe simplicity can help you too, and that's why I wrote this book. It is dedicated to helping you understand who you really are, why you are here, and how that understanding will help you make the most of your current life experience. This book gives you the tools to help you value yourself more, create everyday happiness, and live a truly fulfilling life. These tools are simple and practical. You will discover a blend of common sense and wisdom gleaned from my own life as well as the lives of my clients combined with accessible and nondenominational spiritual insight.

My own journey in life hasn't exactly been a walk in the park, and that's putting it mildly. (I share some of my tougher learning experiences in chapter 3.) However, my clouds have shifted, and I can see their silver lining. My depression and confusion have been replaced with freedom, clarity, and happiness.

If I can make it through the dark tunnel, so can you. That's not to underestimate myself, but simply to state that all of us have options to create a better life. Yes, I know. We live in a world of extremes, and it's not always easy to see the possibilities. Finding authentic happiness and building a better quality of life can seem an impossible dream. But believe me, dreams can become a reality.

I am free and happy now that I have discovered easier ways of dealing with the challenges in my life. Oh yes, I still get my fair share of challenges. We are all on a journey of growth. Sometimes it's the hurdles of everyday life that allow us to grow stronger. I doubt we will ever eliminate our issues completely. However, I have learned how to remain at peace within, even during the hard times. And so can you.

I am excited and, above all, grateful—excited at the thought this book can help you live a "life of a lifetime" and grateful for the opportunity to share your transformational journey with you.

Christoph

CHAPTER 1

The Moment of Awakening

Nothing is the same ever again.

It can occur when you're watching a movie, walking through nature, or listening to music. It can happen when you are home watching television, traveling out of town, or attending a lecture. I have seen it occur at my seminars, during coaching sessions, or in short exchanges with strangers.

It's an extraordinary moment, and it can happen at any point in your life. It's that moment of magic when something inside you shifts. *Forever.*

The shift usually takes place in your mind first. The heart follows later. However, sometimes what you hear, see, or feel is so overwhelmingly powerful that it goes straight to your heart. That's what *resonating* is all about.

So, what is this magical moment? You may call it a "Hmmmm, wait a minute moment," or an "Aha! moment," or the fancier term "Awakening." What you call it doesn't really matter. What does matter is how significant this moment is. It heralds the start of great personal change and growth.

Just the other night I was doing a guided meditation at a wellness center. The event was an introduction to meditation and had attracted a good crowd. At the end of the evening, a woman came to me and said, "I can't thank you enough. I have found myself." When I asked her what she had felt during the meditation, she replied, "The part when you asked us to gently place our hands on our heart and you said, 'Welcome home,' I felt something for the first time in my life. It was as if I encountered myself. I became aware of myself, and I finally got to spend some time with that person. It was weird but incredibly peaceful."

These moments of awakening happen at both the mundane and spiritual levels of your life. I'm sure you can remember a time when you heard a voice on the radio and thought, "I want to know who this is and buy their album." Or maybe you saw a television program about a particular country and thought, "Oh, I want to go there."

It wasn't until later that you discovered these particular events were important for you. Maybe the lyrics of a song prompt you to take a significant action, such as trying something new that then becomes a passion. Or maybe you travel to that country you saw advertised on television and meet the person of your dreams. Most of us relate to these kinds of events, and we call them coincidences. But are they?

Moments of awakening are highly valuable. They cause you to look at yourself and your life with new eyes. They lay the foundation for a newer, lighter you. They set the wheels of transformation in motion. They are the fuel to your soul's engine of continuous evolution, driving the desire to change and expand, empowering you to work on yourself and advance to the next level of awareness and conscious living.

This doesn't mean you have to become a philosopher or even a mystic. Many of you already know that my spiritual work is nondenominational, grounded, and, above all, practical. Every day I meet people who have never heard of spirituality or life coaching, and I enjoy sharing with them what I know and how it can help them. These interactions often trigger a moment of awakening for them, and they begin exploring their life in a deeper way.

Recognizing your moments of awakening is important. Using them wisely is very helpful on your journey through life, no matter what stage of the journey you find yourself in. Whether you are new to conscious living or not, life constantly invites you to begin today, try again, or stretch further.

There's no age limit or other restrictions for spiritual awakening. People young and old, from different world cultures, with diverse occupations and interests all find their way to spirituality and a more consciously aware way of living. You have only to look at the guests at my seminars sitting next to each other to know this is true.

There's never any obligation to walk this path of practical spirituality. You can live a perfectly happy life without ever giving spirituality a single thought. I'm sure you've heard people say, "I just don't have the inspiration" or "Nothing exciting ever happens in my world."

But it does. Inspiration is everywhere. However, seeing it is the challenge. That's where practical spirituality comes in. It shows you how to remain aware and look for guidance,ideas, and insights. It's a tool for life, helping you work with the information you receive and use it for your benefit.

Another reason why moments of awakening are important is because they help you draw a line under your current circumstances so you can move on. It wasn't until I had my moment of awakening that I fully acknowledged I was on the so-called wrong path. Of course there is no such thing as right or wrong when it comes to personal growth, because every experience is valuable. Valuable, of course, doesn't always mean pleasant!

Looking back, I was a young man with a good job as a flight attendant with a handful of people I called my friends. However, knowing what I know now, I can see I was living my life by default. You know—going to work, forever trying to conform to the expectations of society, and doing the same old things with the same old people. Was I in my comfort zone? Yes. Was I comfortable? Hell no!

Even back then, in my heart I knew I wasn't happy with the way my life was going. I felt confused and anxious. Out of sync, that's for sure. But what did in-sync look like for me? If I wanted to become a happier and emotionally stronger person, I knew I was going to have to do something very different and do it soon.

On the outside, I was the life of the party, the clown, always up for a laugh. But I was very insecure on the inside. And I had had enough of that awful feeling. I was getting so sick and tired of examining and worrying about what people had said the night before. Do you know the feeling? It drove me insane. Their words would flash through my mind the next day like nasty PowerPoint slides. "Why did they say that? Was it supposed to hurt me? Did I say something wrong?"

If you go over and over something often enough, it drives you nuts. I knew this was a clear sign of insecurity, but how on earth was I supposed to do something about it? How could I possibly help myself? Would I ever be able to silence those apprehensive voices in my head?

Help!

I was also annoyed with myself for often coming up with the most stupid anecdotes about heaven only knows what in a rather desperate attempt to get attention. Furthermore, my once fantastic relationship with my high school sweetheart girlfriend was about to completely derail. Sounds like I was ready for a change in my life, don't you think? When

I had my first major moment of awakening, it was an experience I'll never forget for as long as I live.

I was employed as airline cabin crew for Sabena, the national airline of Belgium, but I was still living with my parents in a bid to save some money before settling down on my own. In those days, pre-9/11, working for an airline as crew was still a desirable job, and most of the trips and perks were really great.

I remember taking my parents with me on a couple of my layovers, something they adored. My dad was even allowed to sit in the cockpit during a landing in Madrid. My mom still thinks her trip to Chicago with me was one of the highlights of her life. It was a highlight for me too. I didn't actually work that particular flight, but we traveled on very cheap staff tickets in business class all the way to the Windy City. I got to watch my all-time favorite singer, Sarah Brightman, perform live in concert. Oh yes, the perks were great back then!

One of my favorite destinations was Boston, Massachusetts, on the east coast of the United States. What a gorgeous city, offering the perfect mix of American and European culture, art, and vibe. From whale watching to sharing a huge bucket of chicken wings with the whole crew in a sports bar to walking The Freedom Trail (one of America's first historic walking tours), Boston had it all.

U.S. layovers were short. We would arrive late in the afternoon and fly back to Europe the next day in the early evening. But on one occasion I was blessed with a two-day stopover in Boston because of a schedule change by the airline. We stayed in the beautiful Colonnade Hotel, another reason why I enjoyed going to Boston so much. The Colonnade was a hotel where you could really relax properly, and the room service was great. (Nothing beats a crème brulée after a transatlantic flight!)

I remember the crew from Icelandair also used this majestic hotel. The female flight attendants wore large black leather boots, and I always wondered if they actually wore them during the flight. Surely that must have made quite a noise when they walked down the aisle.

Another thing I remember vividly about this hotel was the cute rubber ducky in the bathroom shower, which was always faithfully waiting for me after a tiring flight. It was a desirable collector's item for any crew member!

During this particular Boston layover I decided not to do the usual sightseeing, but went to a nearby mall instead. Actually I was guided to go there, but that's something I didn't realize back then. I may not remember where I've left my collection of rubber duckies from the Colonnade Hotel, but I will forever remember how I was magnetically drawn to a particular bookstore in that shopping mall. I had no idea where I was going or why, but I instinctively knew I had to go inside the shop. Frankly, reading books was the last thing on my mind at that time, but I still felt strongly compelled to look in the Mind-Body-Spirit section (of all places!)

That's when I noticed the book *The Other Side and Back* by controversial author and psychic medium Sylvia Browne. A few days earlier in Belgium, I had seen a very short excerpt from her appearance on the hugely successful American talk show *Larry King Live*. I had been rather intrigued by the spiritual concepts she was discussing, and her television presence had made quite a strong impact on me.

And here I was in Boston, standing right in front of one of her books, even though I had never had the intention to look up her work in a bookstore. I decided there was something spooky about that and ended up buying the book. It was a small paperback, and it looked easy to read. I figured there was no harm in seeing what all the hype was about. After all, if Larry King wants you on his show, there must be something special about you, right?

I didn't leave my hotel room for 2 days. I was spellbound by Sylvia Browne's book. My moment of awakening had arrived. Something really clicked into place for me. After reading just a few chapters of Ms. Browne's book, I felt I had suddenly accepted myself. I didn't necessarily accept the confused person I had been up until then, but I accepted the fact I was worthwhile and deserving. I became aware that I was somebody—a person as much entitled to happiness and self-esteem as anyone else. I felt I had suddenly been given permission to stand up for myself, to talk freely and confidently, to dream big in my life!

Without a doubt, this was my wake-up call to a better life. The book itself was an easy read about taking simple steps to love and respect oneself. But I had long forgotten those important truths, if I had ever even known them in the first place.

At a time in my life when I needed a significant change, I was given a tool that opened my eyes and awakened my spirit. It was absolutely amazing. I remember sighing, smiling, and then crying tears of joy while I was reading. Even though I barely knew who the author was or the controversy that surrounded her, I knew one thing. This book had captured me. I felt understood, reassured, and inspired.

I was inspired to take *action*. And so, in the weeks and months after my glorious Boston trip, I began making real changes. I started to clear the path to a new me. And there was a lot to be cleared. First, I needed to make changes to my behavior. No more acting funny, desperately trying to get attention. I was determined to be more composed and relaxed around people.

This change in attitude produced amazing results almost overnight. I discovered I could make new friends without being a clown. I noticed people were actually attracted to me because they wanted to get to know me. I think it was because I was happy. Being open, honest, and respectful was like taking off a gas mask and breathing normally again. I was finally able to breathe in self-love and authenticity.

Second, clearing the path to a new Christoph—a confident and genuinely happy chap—also meant I needed to change my thinking. Thankfully, another great benefit of my personal awakening was learning how to ditch self-defeating thoughts and replace them with gentle, uplifting, and self-empowering thoughts instead. This took a little bit of practice. I was so used to thinking poorly of myself.

However, beliefs and behavior go hand in hand. So the more I benefited from my new attitude, the easier it was to think better about myself. Dropping my silly, nervous, and unauthentic clown behavior led to establishing genuine connections with people. This, in turn, helped me think of myself as a calmer person than I had been before. Every time this happened, it reaffirmed my belief that I was indeed a calm person, a guy people wanted to be around. And that felt really great because I had always enjoyed sharing fun with people. Now I could share my authentic self and my happiness.

Another benefit of thinking self-empowering thoughts was that I became less attached to other people's opinions. The old Christoph politely agreed with virtually anything anyone said for the sake of being liked or accepted. However, my new way of thinking about myself allowed me to gently but firmly speak up for my own beliefs and opinions. I acquired a mindset of positive and self-appreciating affirmations that I could now draw upon to give me the strength to speak with confidence.

Today, many years after my own awakening, I devote my life to doing what I can to encourage moments of awakening for other people. It is my passion to share the joys and benefits of stepping onto the path of practical spirituality. Nothing brings me more satisfaction than helping someone discover their inner beauty and authentic power. I can't imagine a better job, and I am grateful to be able to use the lessons from my own past to help my clients with their journeys.

Seeing someone leave at the end of a seminar or a personal coaching session with a radiant smile on their face tells me they've experienced an awakening. It's the most wonderful feeling for them and for me. Spirituality is always meant to be practical, to bring joy and happiness to all of us.

My job is to hold up the mirror so that anyone who's ready to do so can look into it and see their divinity in their own reflection. Once someone acknowledges they are worthwhile and deserving of a better life, I help them lock onto their innate skills and talents to go about creating that life.

It also happens that people come to me to be reawakened. Once upon a time, they had been self-confident or felt passionate about their dreams, but somehow along the way they lost sight of their divine spark. The stress of living in today's world caused them to slide back into uncertainty. It takes a lot of courage for someone to identify this rut and ask for help to get out of it. I love helping people reignite the fire of their ambitions and dreams. I will gladly hold up the mirror to reflect their inner light back to them.

Who knows? Perhaps this book will be your moment of awakening. Or reawakening. Maybe there will be something in this book you are holding in your hands right now that will give you the courage to make positive changes in your life, to overcome your particular challenges. Perhaps this book is the start of an incredible journey for you and all those people whose lives you touch.

When you first open yourself up to practical spirituality, challenges are going to arise. It's part of the process. It's also part of the beauty of awakening. Here are some of the challenges you may face and how you can overcome them.

Rapid Change

Things will move very fast for you at the beginning. You may not be aware of it, but you have given a strong sign to the Universe indicating you are ready for the next phase of your life. You will feel both euphoric and overwhelmed at the same time. Don't despair. This is completely normal. After all, everything is new to you. You aren't always going to know straightaway what to do with the flow of energy and inspiration you will be receiving.

You will have a million and one questions, and you may become impatient to discover the answers to all those questions. For now, just trust that those answers will be revealed to you at a time that suits your higher purpose. In the meantime, spend time meditating and being in nature. Keep active. You may want to join a gym class or do something similar to ensure a healthy mind–body balance.

The rapid changes usually last for a few weeks initially. After that, things will slow down and spirituality will probably start to become more of a steady, constant presence in your life. Once you understand what's going on, remain focused and be gentle with yourself.

Losing Old Friends

As you transform, not all of your friends and the people you know will understand what's happening with you. Your renewed energy might feel uncomfortable to them. That's not because they aren't pleased for you. They just won't always know how to respond to your transformation. Your confidence and new outlook on life could appear awkward in their eyes.

Even though you will probably feel wonderful and will want to share your new interests and views with the world, please remember that you cannot change people if they are not ready. The best thing to do is to give them as much love as you can and be patient with them. Allow your friends time to accept the new you.

Some people will naturally drift away from you, and that is okay. It may not feel okay at the time, but you will be strong enough to cope with the loss. You are creating space for new, like-minded souls to come into your world. It was not your deliberate intention to send old friends on their way, so simply wish them well and trust that everything is working out in perfect order.

Loneliness

You will meet fascinating people on your spiritual path, and you will make many wonderful new friends. However, you will also find yourself alone at times, not just physically but also emotionally. This too is quite normal and to be expected for someone who's decided to embark on their journey of personal and spiritual growth. Look for seminars or gatherings organized by mind-body-spirit groups near you. They can become a source of support and guidance and may be just what you need.

Spending time on your own is not a bad thing, however. It's an opportunity to look inside and meditate on what's important to you. Sometimes you will even long to be on your own, away from the drama and stress you no longer need. For example, after sharing lots of my energy with people, I crave time for myself. It's vital for me to make time to unwind and reenergize, or I simply can't do a good enough job next time. Honor yourself, and allow plenty of you-time, but of course don't shut yourself off from the outside world completely. Strike a balance that works for you.

Impatience

When my spiritual quest began, I wanted to have all the answers to all my questions just as soon as possible. I was eager to know what the future would hold for me, and I wanted to move on quickly. There's a good chance you'll experience a similar restlessness, so let me tell you how I learned to deal with it.

The unfolding of your spiritual growth is a matter of divine timing. Everything you need to know will come to you at the right time, at the right place, and in the right way. Again, right is relative, and the way things will happen for you and to you will certainly not always feel right. But they are indeed right in the grand scheme of things.

If you were able to zoom out from your life, you would see how much time you really have. There's no need to turn your life around in 24 hours.

So often we want to rush things. We fear periods of transition when it seems nothing is happening. Some of us will consult just about anyone to find the answers we're seeking, only to end up being told rubbish by fraudulent psychics (for example) that may cause us to be become even more impatient or more confused. Once again, the golden rule is to trust that whatever you need to know will find its way to you.

Summary of This Chapter

- Moments of awakening can catapult your personal transformation.
- There are no limitations such as age, gender, geographical location, or belief system that determine who receives these moments of awakening.
- Awakening helps you become lighter yet stronger.
- Personal transformation is a process, so be patient and kind to yourself.
- Some people will leave your life, but you will make many new spiritual connections.
- Being on your own does not equal feeling lonely.
- Look for like-minded people who can support and guide you.
- Changes will occur quickly at first and then slow down. Always trust the process and stay focused.

Life constantly invites you to begin today, try again, or stretch further.

CHAPTER 2

Your Own Truth

My first book, *Connecting to Your Inner Light*, offered an introduction to practical spirituality and contained over sixty powerful inspirations to help the reader feel better and more supported on their journey through life. I also briefly shared my understanding of the soul, karma, God, the Universe, and the reason for life.

Much to my delight, many readers and seminar guests asked me to expand more on those fascinating topics, and of course, I happily oblige. My heart sings when people express a genuine desire to explore these concepts further. It excites me because I know just how enlightening and beneficial the insight we gain from doing a little research can be.

With this book, I have a great opportunity to share with you my own understanding of these spiritual themes and, more importantly, how that understanding continues to serve me. Every day this awareness helps me deal better with whatever comes my way, easy or hard. It also offers a possible explanation for all the miracles and calamities in our lives.

I say possible because there's something important you should know before we go further.

No one knows it all. By saying this, I don't want to disappoint you but rather protect you. In recent years, the world has seen a spectacular increase in appreciation for nonreligious spirituality, New Age ideas, and holistic methodologies. That's great, and many people have found it helpful when looking for an alternative to organized religion or allopathic medical treatments. However, it is wise to remain cautious and discerning. You can just as easily be fenced in by the new spirituality as by conventional religion. When hype surrounds a product for commercial reasons, the product can potentially lose its original and genuine credibility. Unfortunately, I feel that this is exactly what has happened to the new spirituality within the past decade. There has been a surge in spiritual competition, so to speak, with many teachers claiming their theories and insights are the ultimate truth.

But nobody knows it all. Truth is always subjective. It's a wonderful opportunity for us to decide for ourselves what resonates with our hearts. If you really want to transform yourself and become confident, you need to find what the truth means for *you*. And that will require digging deep.

You can flow into emotional freedom by allowing yourself to explore whatever appeals to you and then see if it actually serves you or not. I know this might feel a bit uncomfortable at first. We're not always accustomed to thinking for ourselves or forming our own opinions when it comes to spirituality. That is why practical spirituality is so near and dear to my heart. We're allowed to be free.

Practical spirituality allows us to live our lives to the full, within a dogma-free framework of universal love, support, abundance, and creative energy. In my work as a spiritual life coach, I immensely enjoy guiding my clients through the maze of different spiritual philosophies to help them gain clarity on what specifically will be helpful to them.

I was christened when I was just four and a half weeks old. For the next fifteen years, I attended church as was expected of me. But because I wasn't really encouraged to make sense of what was being preached, let alone challenge it, I didn't resonate with much of it. Now I can honestly say I feel closer to God than I ever did when I was in church.

Actually, today I feel one with God. Why? Because the wonderful path of practical spirituality has invited me to finally discover what God means to *me*, what heaven means to *me*, what forgiveness means to *me*. I am free to let go of everything I was expected to accept blindly for the rest of my life.

Nor do I accept blindly all that is offered to me on this new journey either. Despite the fact that Sylvia Browne's book was what prompted my moment of awakening, that doesn't mean I need to agree with or believe everything Ms. Browne espouses. Quite the contrary. I am free to be grateful to Ms. Browne, leave behind that with which I don't agree, and continue on my spiritual journey.

I want to encourage you to awaken to your own truths about life. Precisely because of its detachment from religion, spirituality can often become a beautiful addition to your faith. By taking from both religion and spirituality what you resonate with the most, you can blend your faith with practical spirituality and enjoy the best of what both worlds have to offer.

I recently worked with a woman who wanted help with her transition from religion to spirituality. Rather than unnecessarily cutting cords for good, Susan and I found exciting ways to balance the religion in which she'd been raised with her newfound spirituality in a way that worked for her. That's what it's all about—discovering your own truths and shaping them into life tools. Rather than staying stuck in a place of uncertainty, separation, or fear, you can use those tools to help you move forward.

It's important to approach any type of teachings—religious or spiritual—with an open mind. I am a big believer in keeping things real and staying grounded. You are in the driver's seat of your life, and you are always free and empowered to decide if something resonates with you.

From time to time, your views and beliefs may shift somewhat. Please don't let that confuse you or cause you to question your spiritual awakening. As new experiences and what I like to call heart changes come your way, it's only normal to occasionally update your opinions and conclusions accordingly. This is a wonderful and very authentic way to build a beautiful Temple of Wisdom for yourself.

Everything I'm talking about right now is how I understand it at this particular stage of my life. My understanding may and probably will evolve over the course of the coming years, and I certainly want to allow space for that to happen. I want to be sure I'm not fenced in by my own spiritual beliefs. When I look around me, I see many people who adhere to very strict religious concepts and rules. However, the truth is not set in stone. We can and should open our minds to new concepts and beliefs as we move through life. I don't want to be told there is only one way. That's just plain silly and downright frightening. I have my own spiritual teachers and self-help leaders whom I respect, but that doesn't mean I choose to follow everything they advocate.

Practical spirituality is always about finding what works for *you* by doing your research, walking your path, and honoring your feelings along the way. Be leery of anyone who claims to have all the solutions for you. If they can offer something that helps you, great. However, it's even better if you learn how to reach your own conclusions and to bring about change in your world from within. A spiritual teacher merely points you in a certain direction and then encourages you to find out if it is the right direction for you.

My grandfather told me that during both World Wars, churches were overflowing. People were very frightened and looking for protection. I notice an interesting parallel with today's commercialized spirituality. Being human means being vulnerable and going through difficult experiences—breakups, job loss, depression, losing a loved one, living with no sense of direction. When we feel sad or lost, we are likely to look for just about anything we think can help us. We may feel drawn to strong (and usually loud) spiritual messengers with seemingly perfect lives. We risk becoming too dependent upon them and what they are espousing. We accept new beliefs and so-called truths in order to make it through a dark phase of our lives.

This dynamic is understandable but, at the same time, sad and sometimes even dangerous. Different things work for different people. We all have the freedom to choose what we want to believe, who we listen to, and who we hire to advise and guide us. I want people to be free to decide what will help them and what won't. And of course I want people to be happy. However, what concerns me is how perfectly sane, hardworking people are being brainwashed by spiritual gurus. I believe that's an indication that those people haven't yet arrived at the place on their spiritual path where they begin to think for themselves.

It's a vulnerable place to be, and unscrupulous so-called spiritual gurus can take advantage of that vulnerability. I frequently receive calls and e-mails from people concerned about what a specific guru has said. "She told me not to make important decisions during the full moon." "He said my disability was a punishment from God." "She said my relationships fail because I was a bad person in a past life."

I know many people feel somewhat lost without a set of rules to guide them, but the truth is there are no rules when it comes to your spiritual growth. None at all. And that's not one of my rules by the way. Rather, it's another invitation to remember your complete freedom in this matter. Control, dogma, and fear have no place within practical spirituality. As I have said before and will continue repeating, no one knows it all. What a teacher (or anyone else for that matter, including myself) shares is his or her own personal truth. What is true for someone else and what serves someone else, even if the message was received from a higher source, has been filtered through that person's own belief system—for the better, but not always.

What religious or spiritual beliefs have you held for years that no longer resonate with you in your heart and soul? What beliefs do you wish you could let go of? Write down your answer on a piece of paper and save it. Later in the book, we will use your answer to help you release these beliefs.

Throughout my own spiritual development, I have always been fascinated by our reason for living. And I'm very grateful that the universe has brought me many wonderful people, books, and other study materials that have helped me learn about this topic. I learned how we are, in fact, not just human beings but also (and more importantly) souls. We are souls having an experience of life in the form of human beings. Some say we are spiritual beings having a human experience.

Oh dear. Another theory? Perhaps. Has it been helpful to me? Absolutely. It is the most important insight I've had to date, and it has changed everything in my life. If it can do that for me, it can do that for you! I am hugely excited by that potential, aren't you?

But please remember that this is my belief. Of course I will do my best to convey how I understand and work with this information, but you are invited to listen to your heart while I do so. As is often the case with anything to which you're exposed that may be new or different, allow yourself some time to digest the information and reflect upon it.

God as Paper

I want you to imagine a piece of paper. Poster size would be good. Imagine that this paper represents God, or whichever Presence or Higher Power with which you feel comfortable. If you don't really believe in God or your faith has a different name for this power, that's absolutely fine. Please choose whatever works for you. Perhaps you could call it *Universe* for the purposes of this visualization.

Now start decorating this piece of paper in your mind's eye. Make it the most beautiful, awe-inspiring poster you've ever seen. Be creative.

Make it colorful, vibrant, a different size if you wish. Notice how it beckons to you with all its incredible features. The energy it emits is astonishing. You feel extremely drawn to it. All you want is to be a part of it. You want to be absorbed in its power and beauty and become one with it. Both the poster and you are now one and the same. You are unified.

Now, think back to what you decided to call your poster. Let's say you chose Universe. Can you see what just happened during our little meditation? First you acknowledged the Universe. Then you yearned to become a part of it. And then you did!

Now imagine taking a tiny part of your poster. Pretend it is you. Are the sizes of the tiny piece and the large poster different? Of course they are. But is there a difference in substance between them? Not at all. And there we have it.

I often use this exercise during my seminars. It allows participants to conjure up an image of God that's uniquely theirs and with which they can resonate. It's a simple but thought-provoking way to suggest that we are indeed a part of the Universe (or God or Higher Power or . . .). You may have heard this before, or perhaps this is the first time you're being exposed to this concept. Either way, give yourself time to absorb and reflect upon this idea.

Here's what I believe. I believe you and I and everyone else split off from the Universal Source, and we're all on a phenomenal journey. We are all tiny but precious parts of the poster. Every physical body is linked with a soul, and every soul was once born from the Source. That includes friend and foe, rich and poor, healthy and sick, sinners and saints.

How do you feel about this message? How do you feel about the idea that a so-called bad person is also a part of the Universal Source, also on a spiritual journey? A difficult message to accept? Yes, it is at first. However, it's important to be aware that you are not taking on the same behavior or thoughts as that person. You both may originate from the same soul source, but you have each decided to be a very different, very individual expression of that source. It is that difference in expression, that difference in individuality that makes you who you are and the "bad" person who he/she is.

I believe that difference doesn't mean that we aren't all the same and that we aren't all an integral part of God. When viewed from the level of original creation, we are. By the way, here's something you might want to try the next time you pray. Replace the word "God" with your own name. It's quite startling, and a powerful awakening to your own divinity.

So exactly how does this belief help me in my life? Why am I excited about all this? What's the advantage of looking at people through a spiritual lens of oneness? Because it greatly enhances the quality of my life. It contributes to my emotional freedom, and that makes me feel better. It's as simple as that. By applying the knowledge that all souls, along with their aspirations, come from the same Source, I have learned how to look at people with new eyes, to react to them differently. I have been able to release the need to criticize or gossip. I no longer jump to conclusions. I can detach from people and their opinions more easily. I can understand people and their motives better, and that helps me avoid unnecessary conflict. I can see why people do the things they do, why they make the choices they make, and why they say the things they say. It enables me to be a better communicator and a better coach.

A while ago, a good friend of mine wanted to talk to me about her fiancé. Apparently he had been rather sharp to her during a heated conversation about their upcoming wedding. She wanted to vent and complain about him with me. I could have easily sympathized with her and fallen for the "poor you" approach, but I didn't. I decided to focus on the bigger picture here instead—two souls experiencing the ups and downs of a romantic relationship. I wanted to turn what could potentially be an ugly gossip session into a more constructive, heartfelt talk with my friend.

That doesn't mean I ignored my friend's emotional pain or decided to entertain her with a lecture on the origin of souls. All I had to do was gently remind her about the two sides of the coin—that her fiancé, just like her, is a beautiful soul on a journey of growth. Sometimes people react in surprisingly different ways when they are under a lot of stress, such as an upcoming wedding and the realization that they are making a lifetime commitment.

The benefits of zooming out a little bit once in a while and seeing everyone as a divine soul on a journey are endless. In recent years, I have become a calmer person, and my patience has been noticed by many. People ask, "Chris, how do you manage to stay so calm? Doesn't he/she get on your nerves?"

I reply that other people's behavior affects me significantly less because now I see them as souls, not as people with power over me. It's like watching people's interactions and the unfolding of life around me from behind a beautiful screen of empathy, spiritual understanding, and calmness.

This is particularly useful when we have to be around people we are not fond of. Last Christmas I was in Belgium to spend quality time with my family, when I was invited by an old friend to come to a Christmas party at her house. I knew other people would be there who hadn't always been nice to me, and some of them had been downright offensive. However, because of her time constraints, I also knew this would be my only opportunity to spend time with my dear friend.

The old Christoph would never have considered going to the party. I would have been afraid of nasty remarks from those negative people and going home feeling like I was a total mess. However, the new Christoph remembered that those events took place many years ago and that he wasn't as fazed by other people's opinions anymore.

I enthusiastically attended the party. I focused on catching up with my friend and having a wonderful time. I adopted a more neutral attitude toward the other guests, who seemed surprised by it and by my general demeanor of happiness. They actually came over to me to see what my happy vibe was all about!

My friend phoned me the next day to tell me how amazed she had been by the difference in my attitude. She had noticed and enjoyed my high levels of confidence and self-esteem, and she told me it had made the party extra special for her. Her compliment was an extraordinary Christmas gift I hadn't been expecting!

Of course all this doesn't mean I always agree with people or approve of their actions. Being on a path of practical spirituality isn't about becoming everybody's best friend. But seeing people as unique souls does make my life easier because I manage to shift from feeling bothered to creating a sense of calm in my mind. This allows me to interact with someone in a far less defensive manner.

The next time someone annoys you, look just above their head and imagine a beautiful tiny white light there. As you listen to them going on (and on and on!), focus on the little light radiating love and tranquility. I promise you will be much less affected by their draining energy. In fact, you are now focusing on the Higher Self of that person. On this soul level, you communicate with loving thoughts rather than words. The person's Higher Self will decide whether or not to absorb the thoughts you are sending. However, if you do it with good intent, it usually will. You will notice a difference in the person's demeanor. I use this tool all the time, and I find it very helpful.

Think of a challenging person in your life. What is the core issue, and what would you like to see change? Put the book down for a moment. Close your eyes and visualize this person. Give yourself a few seconds to allow any initial hard feelings to ease away. When you are in that space of calm, picture the little bright light of the person's soul. Talk to it. Introduce yourself. Share your intentions. You will be surprised how much easier things will be the next time you see the individual.

So Far, Soul Good!

Now that we have taken a closer look at where all souls originate from, let's also talk about why they decide to embark on a journey. Surely the Universal God Source is a pretty wonderful place to be, so why did we make that audacious decision to detach for a while and take on human form? Discovering the answer to this mystery has been very helpful to me when I've struggled to make sense of my life. In fact, this may be the only answer you or I ever need.

Every single one of us or, more accurately, every single one of our souls makes a deliberate choice to experience life. We incarnate (take on physical form) for a very good reason. When we are in the Universal God Source, we possess all the knowledge we could ever wish for. Remember how we discovered that we are a part of an all-knowing God? Therefore, our souls are all-knowing. The main reason why a soul decides to take on the miraculous project of coming "down" to Earth is to undergo that which it already knows but hasn't yet experienced.

Expertise (knowledge) and experience don't necessarily equate. Just because you know something doesn't mean you've had the opportunity to experience it. For example, I could talk to you for hours about the beauty of South Africa. However, if I've never been there physically, how can I fully understand and appreciate the smell of the bush or the magic of the gorgeous landscapes or tell you how it feels to watch a sunset from the top of Table Mountain?

It's the experience of *beingness* (taking on form as a human) that adds an extra dimension and depth to the soul's wisdom. Every soul wants to *be*. It's through *being* that our soul keeps evolving. The deliberate choice to take on life in a human form allows the soul to fulfill its wish list. As you might imagine, this beingness offers the perfect conditions and situation for the soul to experience a variety of states and circumstances.

Let's take a look at our lives. What are we choosing to discover during our time here? I say choosing because, contrary to popular belief, not everything in our life is predestined. We can always start over or make changes, and we are certainly not on a track that is fixed or that we can't get off. Here's a relevant question from a reader of my newsletter and my response to him.

Chris, is everything in my life set in stone? Does it all come down to fate? Is it even worth making an effort?

Tom, Manchester, UK

Dear Tom,

You're asking some very valid questions here. The purpose of life, predestination, and the degree to which you have an influence on your life are important topics for everyone. I would love to share my thoughts with you.

I believe we do indeed (as souls) choose our life's blueprint before we are born. We will pick certain things we wish to experience during our life on Earth—some events in more detail than others, depending on the learning opportunity. After all, trying to figure it all out is often a huge learning opportunity in itself.

We are a part of the God Source or Universe or whatever you wish to call it. This Source is all-knowing, but when you split off as an individual soul, you take on one or more lifetimes to experience that which you already know but forget when you incarnate. That's why life really is an invitation to remember that which you've forgotten.

To experience something is always the best way to learn. I could describe to you in detail a specific food prepared in a specific way, but you will want to taste it yourself to experience what it's really like. It's the same thing when it comes to life. Your soul really does want to be here, even though we can't always appreciate that fact because of the challenges we face. Your soul experiences life on behalf of the Universal God Source, and that's wonderful indeed. It's something to be very proud of, so please never ever put yourself down! You are one amazing being on a fascinating journey.

But—and this is a very big but—even though you chose the general outline of your life, there is a great deal of room for maneuvering! I believe you cocreate your life. Some parts of it are predestined by your soul's choices before birth, but other parts are determined by the decisions you make during your life. You do have free will, and you can influence the course of things, but only to a certain degree. After all, if your soul picked it from the menu, you will want to experience it anyway, sooner or later.

So that means the purpose of life is to exist. By doing so, you also automatically fulfill your soul's desire to explore its blueprint. Every event, every challenge helps your soul expand and evolve. Things may feel good or bad, but ultimately they just are. They are neutral. As a human you attribute feelings and meanings and judgments to experiences. Your soul (your Higher Self) doesn't.

The most horrible events in our lives become easier to understand and accept when we remember why we are going through them. Again, some events will be very painful and others joyous, but every experience helps us grow spiritually. It often helps me snap out of the victim role when I remember what's happening. My soul chose the experience.

So I might as well experience it now and leave it behind me. That's why I'm ready to accept it more readily and move forward more quickly without the unnecessary drama.

> Life is like going to the grocery store with your shopping list. Sometimes you get distracted and decide to pick up different items rather than the ones on your list. That doesn't mean you can't enjoy those items you picked up. It just means you'll have to run back to the store eventually to get the items that were on your soul's original wish list.
>
> Best regards,
> Christoph

Summary of This Chapter

- Practical spirituality encourages you to discover and follow your own truths about life.
- Your views and opinions will occasionally change, which is entirely normal. Build a solid Temple of Wisdom for yourself.
- You are always free and empowered to choose what you believe.
- You are an integral part of the Universal God Source.
- You are a soul having an experience of life by taking on a human form.
- Your soul has a self-chosen wish list that serves as the blueprint for your life.
- Flowing into emotional freedom becomes a reality when you learn to see the events, people, and circumstances in your life as opportunities for personal and spiritual growth. Every single experience contributes to the evolution and expansion of your soul.

We are, in fact, not just human beings, but also (and more importantly) souls. We are souls having an experience of life in the form of human beings. We are spiritual beings having a human experience.

CHAPTER 3

Leaving the Dark Behind

It started with a cheeky suggestion. When I told a friend of mine I was planning to write a new book, he looked at me with an impudent grin on his face. "You ought to include a dark chapter," he said. "Obviously your readers will expect the book to be all about uplifting stuff, so why don't you give them a little surprise by adding a chapter about your gloomy personal experiences?"

We had a good laugh about that, and I thanked him for his suggestion. However, I didn't dismiss his idea altogether. As I was drafting my book, I knew it would be useful for you if I included some of the more painful experiences I had been through in my life.

Have you ever noticed how we start feeling a little bit better the minute we find out other people are dealing with challenges similar to ours? It's almost as if we're saying to ourselves, "Thank God I am not the only one who's going through this!" It reassures us.

Have you ever been on a job interview, and you were so nervous you almost felt sick? But then you met the other candidates and discovered they felt the same way. It probably put your mind at ease, and you probably felt better about the interview, knowing the others were as paralyzed by their fears as you were.

Is it selfish to react this way? I don't believe so. I think its okay as long as we use it to help us deal with our own issues. After all, isn't that why support groups are so successful? They generate a feeling of belonging and security in participants, enabling them to learn from each other and move on.

The same goes for television soap operas and movies. Relating to a fictional character's issues can help us better deal with our own. Just the other day I was coaching a man in his late forties who was divorced and had worked all of his life as the only mechanic in a small factory that had ceased operating. Danny had been made redundant and his confidence was gone. He came to me to explore his options and rebuild his self-esteem.

Halfway during our session, Danny said, "You know, Christoph, I feel like that man in that movie—what's his name again? Will Smith! He played that homeless guy whose wife had left him and he was struggling to find a decent job."

Danny was referring to the brilliant inspirational movie *The Pursuit of Happiness*, starring Will Smith. Danny clearly recognized himself in the scenario and could relate to the lead character's ordeal. Danny added, "But he made it in the end, didn't he?"

"He sure did," I replied.

"Well then, I guess I'll just have to figure out a way to make it too," declared Danny.

I admired Danny's optimism and attitude. Being made redundant can cause enormous stress, and it's very challenging to remain positive, especially if you have low self-confidence. We spent the rest of our coaching session exploring some of Danny's long-held ambitions and dreams he wants to pursue and discussing the potential challenges and obstacles on his path.

Gradually, Danny seemed to find his confidence, and he came up with some good solutions. However, sometimes he'd get stuck and need a little inspiration. When that happened, all I had to do was ask him, "What would Will Smith do?" Almost immediately, Danny would think of a resolution to the problem, and that would boost his confidence even more. We can gain so much from relating to someone else's hurdles in life. It can give us the reassurance, inspiration, and motivation we need. This is especially the case when we look up to someone who has managed to overcome their problems. Riding through the storms in our lives becomes easier when we look at how others rose to the challenges in their lives.

Do you remember Sarah Brightman, the singer whose music I so admired, and Sylvia Browne, who wrote the book that inspired my moment of awakening? They have encouraged millions of people with their singing and writing talents, respectively, and have received international acclaim. But they have also been the targets of vicious attacks by their critics. On more than one occasion, the media has criticized each of them harshly.

Both women have also experienced considerable challenges in their private lives away from the limelight.

However, they have climbed their mountains gracefully and have found a way to pull through by focusing on sharing their gifts with the world and using the joy those gifts bring to motivate themselves to keep charging forward.

I admire both women. They have been a source of strength for me. Their lives and careers have often kept me grounded and motivated. They have inspired me to trust my instincts, develop my people skills, and honor my own personal style. I can honestly say I have learned a great deal about being resilient and following my dreams by looking at how these women have done the same.

Similarly, by sharing how I have navigated some steep learning curves in my life, my purpose is to assist you on your journey. I know we can overcome darkness. I know there's always a better way to handle our suffering and uncertainty. I know there's a light at the end of the tunnel. I love the analogy of the beautiful lotus flower that begins its existence in dull mud but keeps reaching for the light until finally it breaks the surface of the pond and blossoms. Helping people believe there is always a way forward and a solution to their current circumstances, that they really can bring changes into their life, is the source of great joy for me. In fact, it's the driving energy behind my spiritual coaching work.

During my seminars, I always talk openly about my past. I've noticed people seem pleasantly surprised by that. I've been told it's refreshing to hear someone talk openly about his challenges rather than pretending life is a walk in the park. In fact, during a recent seminar, I was asked to include some of my stories when I wrote this book, and so I have.

Growing Up in My Brother's Shadow

My childhood was challenging. I grew up in the shadow of my superstar brother Philip, who was 7 years older than me. That's a significant age gap, especially during childhood and those roller-coaster teenage years. Frankly, it's a recipe for disaster, or at least it was for us.

As much as we appreciate each other today and I am the godfather of Philip's beautiful daughter, we didn't exactly click when we were younger.

Looking back, I suppose it couldn't have been any different. Philip was a bright young man, enjoying life and love, and sailing through school. I, on the other hand, was the little brother who was always "there"— there as in the way, as in not smart enough, as in a nuisance to Philip.

My brother was the wise and handsome one while I was the creative one who was always a bit odd and who struggled with school. From my parents' perspective, I would imagine raising Philip was fairly easy, whereas having a kid like me was a challenge because I was so different from my brother. While my brother would be reading or studying or assembling model cars, I was dressing up as my latest movie hero or sneaking off to the nearest amusement park or parading on a carnival float. I felt under constant pressure at home. I had to compete with my brother and prove myself. As far as my parents were concerned, Philip was doing all the right things, and I felt I had to achieve the same, be the same, and walk in his footsteps. It was an awful situation, and I recall spending a lot of time alone in my room.

All the praise and attention always seemed to go to my brother. I was forever trying to get noticed. Unfortunately, the way I went about it was foolish. I would regularly take my brother's precious belongings and hide them or even break them, especially his expensive model cars. I certainly got a lot of attention that way—in the form of punishment, of course. However, it was attention nonetheless, and we humans often go to great lengths for it. As you can imagine, Philip and I spent many years not being exactly the best of friends, to put it mildly. When I came of age, thankfully things changed for the better, and our relationship slowly became more positive. I had matured and began minding my own business. Philip was offered his first job and moved out of the family house. Now there was breathing space for me and less need to prove myself to my parents. My parents and I had more time together, just the three of us, and I became calmer and dropped my mischievous, attention-seeking behavior.

Today my brother and I have found common ground and get along famously. But it's been a long process. It has taken a lot of time for the emotional wounds from our constant fighting in the past to heal. Philip is married with children and lives in Brussels. Whenever I go to Belgium to visit my parents, I make sure to visit Philip and his family. We always have a great time, and it is also a lovely opportunity for me to see my wonderful goddaughter and her brothers.

After many years doing my research into spirituality, I have learned that Philip's and my connection was an agreement between our souls to be brothers in this lifetime. As I am writing this, the energy flowing through me is so strong I can almost feel the Universe whispering in my ear, "Of course it was!"

I continue to have a high regard for my brother, and he's happy I've found my way in life as well. A few years ago, Philip was in the audience at one of my life coaching presentations. It was a lecture entitled, "8 Steps to Daily Happiness," and I had invited him to come along to check out what my work was about. It was so good to see him sitting there, enjoying listening to what I was sharing with the audience. Later I found out he even put some of my coaching tips into practice. I remember feeling such a strong sense of accomplishment and pride, as if my heart were shouting, "Look, I am worthy, I can achieve things too!"

Maybe you find yourself living in the shadow of a sibling and feeling inferior. If this is the case, try zooming out to get a broader view of what may seem like a hopeless situation. By zooming out, I mean keeping an open mind and exploring the spiritual meaning behind the situation. This practice is very powerful when we want to make more sense of the connections we have with the people in our lives.

In the previous chapter, I discussed how all of us are souls on a journey. Sometimes those souls nudge one another a little. Consider the possibility that you and your siblings made a spiritual arrangement— an agreement—to spend time together here on Earth. Before you incarnated, your souls decided on the challenges you would create for each other. I'm sure my brother and I said, "Let's experience not getting along during the first fifteen years of our lives." This way Philip learned to cope with an annoying little brother who wanted to be the center of attention, and I had the opportunity to figure out a way to reach adulthood in one piece emotionally.

"All the world's a stage," Shakespeare once wrote. Well, that's certainly true for our souls when they take on human form. During our lifetimes they have countless self-chosen opportunities to experience a myriad of sibling issues that allow our souls to grow. And as many of us know, those issues can sometimes be rather dramatic, if not downright theatrical!

Summer Camp Abuse

At age 10, my soul was blessed with a hefty learning experience. It's only now that I'm able to call the sexual abuse I endured a blessing. It took place while I attended a summer camp for children in the Swiss Alps, and it continued for 2 years until I finally gathered enough courage to speak out about it.

My spiritual growth has enabled me to recognize and accept what happened and why it happened. Because I am proud of myself for coming to terms with what happened to me and, more importantly, because I suspect many of you have been through a similar ordeal, I have no problem talking about my experience.

What I am about to explain is the result of years of studying the journey of the soul. It is not something you read about once and say, "Oh, now I understand. I totally agree!" Of course not, because it takes time to fully understand the spiritual logistics behind what are often very cruel and harmful acts.

I believe my soul planned to and agreed to undergo the experience of being in a life (and thus in a body) where sexual abuse would occur in order to learn and evolve. It seems that my circumstances at home and the fact I was a lost and confused child were a perfect setup for this kind of experience to take place.

In addition, I am convinced that it happened in such a way that it allowed many other souls to learn from it as well. The souls of my abuser, my parents, and the other people who became involved when I brought everything to light learned from my experience in a way that benefited the evolution of their souls. The experience has certainly played a significant role in my life. I'm grateful that practical spirituality proved to be extremely helpful to me once more. It was a much-needed tool that helped me process the experience and its lessons.

Discovering practical spirituality has helped me see everything from an angle of ongoing spiritual learning, growing, and then moving on. Would there be any purpose for me to stay stuck in the victim position? Of course not. Is there any need to feel hatred toward my abuser? No. There would be only one person who would suffer from that—me. Recognizing these two truths became the foundation for my emotional healing.

Why would I choose to walk through life hating someone? Imagine the enormous stress that would cause me. Just think how my mind and body would be affected by that. I would never be able to trust people again. My ability to share my love and intimacy with those who deserve it would be greatly affected. That was an option I did not choose for my future. Instead, I chose to respect myself and rebuild my self-worth.

In addition, I don't believe worrying about or deciding upon the type of punishment for my abuser's actions is my responsibility. That's up to the authorities. Now that his soul has had the experience, I sincerely hope the abuser is in no position to come into contact with other young children. That's all that matters to me. The soul agendas have been served. I have moved on. Today I use my experience of sexual abuse as an important tool in my coaching toolbox, helping other victims of abuse come to terms with their pasts so they too can move on with their lives and live in freedom.

Bullied at School

As if I weren't lonely enough at home (my parents were busy people and often had to attend social functions), my life became more of a nightmare when I was in my third year of secondary school in Belgium. I began to be bullied.

The word "hell" comes to mind here. I had to avoid the other children if I wanted to escape the mean comments and the never-ending threat of being beaten up. I had to take a different bus or walk the long way home. I had to pretend to be sick sometimes so I could stay home and avoid the torment at school.

The horror called "being bullied" lasted only 1 year, but I can assure you that the emotional imprint was very hard to erase. People frequently say, "Kids can be so cruel," and I can certainly attest to that. Add the bullying to the frequent encounters with my summer camp abuser and the general lack of support around me, and suffice it to say that was a very challenging period in my life.

The first day of the next school year, I decided enough was enough. I wanted to be able to enjoy school again. I knew I was a cool kid to be around, and I was prepared to do anything to prove that to my fellow students. I was ready to speak up for myself.

What a feeling! To this day I remember my "they aren't going to get me this time" attitude, and it worked. I was left alone. No kicks, no insults, no gossip. It's amazing what can happen when we empower ourselves by refusing to be victims. From then on, my interactions with other students began to change. School was once again a good place to be.

Today I realize the tremendous value of this bullying experience. Not only has my soul learned about pain and suffering, I can now better help clients who come to me with similar bullying issues. It happens more frequently than you might think. Many people suffer from workplace-related peer pressure. A quick search on the Internet reveals that literally millions of people are bullied at work.

Are you in a similar position? Are you subjected to bullying or harassment at work or elsewhere? Then I encourage you to do the following. First, consider discussing your predicament with a designated employee representative from the Human Resources Department or your trade union. Make a formal complaint if necessary. Second, if you are a sensitive person and/or you are afraid to take action, just keep reading.

Consider for a moment that you are going through these harsh experiences for a really good reason. Imagine there's sense behind all the intimidation, fear, and embarrassment in your life. Think how much easier it could be to overcome all this if you understood why you find yourself in this situation in the first place.

When we become aware of the underlying reasons for the events in our lives, we are given the key that opens the doors to positive change. Your beautiful soul is here on a journey of expansion. It longs to learn and develop, and it does so through you. You are the one making it all possible. You are the carrier for this miracle. Your soul took on the challenge of experiencing bullying and suppression, and you are living this experience on behalf of your soul. That's something to be very proud of because you are brave and committed to helping your soul expand. In other words, you are much stronger and more precious than you might think. Your contribution in this metaphysical process is of tremendous value and significance. Now, if you read this and think to yourself, "Well, I've certainly experienced enough," that's a clear sign you are ready to draw the line. You are about to unlock the doors to positive change and slam them wide open! But to gain the confidence to do that, you need to consider one more thing. This may be the perfect time for you to overcome your current situation and reap an additional benefit.

Spiritual learning opportunities are always twofold. You learn and grow twice—once by undergoing the harsh experience and once by overcoming it. You certainly don't need to accept being bullied forever. But sometimes you need to undergo a certain experience first in order to learn how to get out of it.

If you feel you've had enough of the learning experience of bullying and it's time for a real change, then step into your Universe-given power and break free. I'm not saying it's easy, but I am saying it's possible. I did it. It is surreal that as a child I was scared to walk past a group of kids at school, and today I speak in front of large groups of people.

If I did it, you can do it. Make a decision to leave the bullying behind you. Realize the harassment has served its purpose, and it is time to move on. If you allow yourself to be respected and valued by people for who you truly are, it will happen. We cocreate our reality. If you say to the Universe, "I can do that!" the Universe will respond, "Yes indeed!"

You will notice an increase in your emotional strength, confidence, and self-esteem. Your radiance and positive attitude will attract the change you are longing for. The people causing you disturbance will no longer feel the need to harass you when you radiate self-respect. They will realize their childish behavior has no impact on you any longer, and they'll quickly give it up.

You will enjoy a bonus from your newfound confidence. New people will feel drawn to you. They will want to get to know this happy, positive person who's shining so brightly. It's a wonderful and genuine way of making new connections. Cocreation is a very powerful process so make sure to keep an eye on your overall behavior and thinking, because it will greatly influence your life. When I look back on my bullying experience, I have come to understand that we often attract precisely that which we *don't* want. As a child, of course I didn't know about this metaphysical dynamic, but today I'm sure my insecure attitude and defeated behavior to some degree contributed to the reasons I was bullied. After all, I made the evasive choices to take the other bus, walk by myself, and stay at home.

Do you see what I mean? Sometimes we have to snap out of a behavior that no longer serves us. There are many wonderful ways to catch people's attention, and playing the poor me card isn't one of them. Know that you deserve genuine respect, but only you can make that happen. When you accept that you are *allowed* to feel free and happy and when you change your behavior and outlook on life accordingly, you will naturally gain positive attention from others. Honor and value yourself. Expect more uplifting interactions with those around you. You are worth loving, and others will benefit from what you have to offer.

Before we continue, I do want to clarify that, despite the profound learning experiences I talked about earlier, I did experience happiness as a youth. My childhood contained a good deal of laughter, friendship, partying, good health, traveling, and love. However, today my definition of happiness is very different from my definition of happiness back then. Today I experience a genuine happiness and inner peace—far more satisfying and consistent than the happiness I enjoyed as a child because I was having fun or partying.

No Direction in Life

My next big learning experience is something that seems to be a significant challenge for many people. It's the pivotal question we all have to ask ourselves at some point, "What do I want to do with my life?"

It was certainly the question playing on my mind when I was having a hard time at university in Antwerp, Belgium. To make a long story short, my time at university wasn't my finest hour. I had some excellent scores on my psychology and sociology exams, but that was about it. I had no idea what I wanted to study or what I wanted to do with my life. Even today I wonder how on earth someone is supposed to make an informed decision about what to study at the ripe old age of 18. It's insane if you ask me.

The only thing I vaguely knew about myself was that I enjoyed "doing good" for people, plus I had always been fascinated by the map of the world. (Not exactly your main entry requirements for university!) The real reason I enrolled in university was to follow in the footsteps of my father and, you've guessed it, my brainy brother. Of course that was just a misguided attempt to copy their achievements. The only thing I copied successfully was the partying associated with being a student, and I'm pretty sure I outdid them in that subject.

I can joke now about what I excelled at, but it wasn't so amusing when I left university and had to go to work in a warehouse. I remember getting into my mum's car on that cold October morning, tears in my eyes, knowing that all my university friends were still on campus. They were very good at their chosen subjects, and they were having a great time.

But I wasn't on campus with my friends now. I was living with my parents, and I had absolutely no idea where to go or what to do next. If university had been hell, believe me when I say this felt a hundred times worse. I had to deal with my feelings of guilt, shame, disappointment, and anger.

Days at the warehouse seemed endless. The atmosphere was grim. I was working alongside depressed and frustrated men and women who could talk only about television and their next cigarette break. I managed to carry on for a couple of months, but it wasn't exactly a happy Christmas that year. As my parents' house wasn't too far from Antwerp, I would make frequent visits to my friends at university on my days off. It was always something to look forward to, and I enjoyed driving because it gave me time to think about my life and what I could do to get it back on track. It was during one of those drives that I was listening to a CD from the musical *Jekyll & Hyde*. When the song *A New Life* came on and I heard, "A new life, what I wouldn't give to have a new life," I started to cry.

I had hit rock bottom. I had no purpose, no goals, no dreams—nothing. I slowed down, turned the car around, and headed back home. I was having a complete emotional breakdown, and I didn't want my friends to see me like this.

One evening I was smoking a cigarette outside my parents' house (an unhealthy habit I was eventually able to quit). The divine timing of the Universe must have been right for me to receive an important ray of light in what seemed like eternal darkness. Here's what happened.

It was another one of those moments when I felt completely isolated from the world. I remember thinking for the thousandth time, "What do I really, really want to do with my life?" As usual, no answer came. Rather than accepting that awful feeling of disappointment I had gotten so used to, this time I followed my first question by another one. I asked myself, "What do I really, really *enjoy?*" That must have been a much easier question because my heart instantly responded with "traveling."

Hmm, good point. I did indeed enjoy traveling and had been fortunate enough to travel by plane a few times. I kept the inner dialogue going. "I like airplanes. Who are those people who work onboard and serve the food? Surely that must be an actual job, a profession. How do I get in? Where do I start looking?"

Unlike my usual frustrating self-talk, this time my questions must have been the right ones because they were heard by the Universe. Within days I found a brochure on courses to take after secondary school. It was a very comprehensive guide and covered not only the usual higher education options, but also shorter ones in many different fields. Hidden in this gift, I found something that would, at long last, give me wings—literally. I spotted a training course to become airline cabin crew for Sabena, the national airline of Belgium. The course was only 10 weeks long—what a relief to this school-weary young man who up until then had thought his only option was a four-year-long battle at university.

My sights set on a high-flying career (pardon the pun), I researched this amazing job prospect. It was clear to me that my talent for being good with people and my fascination with the world map could be combined in this job. It was perfect! I applied for the next new recruits course and was invited to an assessment day. My first real job interview!

I failed of course. I didn't even make it past the introduction stage. It was all over for me by lunchtime. Who was I kidding? All the other candidates had a degree and experience and spoke a second language. I had nothing.

Yes, I was disappointed. But no, I refused to go back to rock bottom. I was determined to become a flight attendant and nothing would stop me. I successfully managed to reverse the negative energy. I took French classes and used the feedback from the interview to prepare me for another assessment day—this time for a low-cost airline that was also based in Brussels. It wasn't quite as glamorous as working for Sabena, but I wasn't in a position to be picky. My efforts were rewarded when I landed the job (another pun!) a few months later.

The crew training course was very enjoyable, and it felt really great to be doing something real for once. This was a proper job, with a good pay check, a nice uniform, and all the other perks and benefits. After a long dark period, I felt much better, and my feelings of self-worth began to come back. I had also learned about contemplation, patience, and perseverance. My soul had chosen to experience all this by me undergoing this experience, and my soul evolved as a result.

No matter how hard the circumstances, we should never give up. There is always a way, a solution that's perfect for us. We need to believe in the divine timing of the Universe and trust that what we need to know or to have will come to us eventually. It will be delivered to us in ways we can't predict and precisely when our soul is ready. It's a matter of faith.

Even when I was at rock bottom, I knew deep inside that one day there would be a solution. I kept on believing that somewhere there was something that would give me the opportunity to expand on what I was already good at and interested in. There are always things we can do to make the waiting more productive—taking language classes, working with a personal coach, doing volunteer work, joining a gym to get fit—to name just a few.

My beloved grandfather used to say to me, "One day at a time." You know what? Those words are so very true. Now I understand that every day spent worrying about the future is a day wasted. But a day spent reflecting and expanding on what already works for us is a day of enlightenment and progression.

Job Loss, Bankruptcy, and Moving

I was really enjoying my first career as airline cabin crew, and I was learning a great deal in a very short space of time. Life was good again, and the Universe had a big surprise in store for me. Sabena was hiring experienced crew members! I jumped at this incredible opportunity and was determined to succeed. My increased self-confidence must have shone through because I was offered the job. I could hardly believe it. I was now working for the Belgian national carrier, and, in a way, I was glad I had failed the initial interview a year earlier. The timing seemed much better because I had matured during that year.

Working in the airline business felt great. After just 1 year of flying short-haul routes, I was accepted to join Sabena's crew that operated on intercontinental flights. What an absolutely amazing experience! To this day, I maintain that my job with Sabena taught me more about the world, its cultures, and its people than any university ever could.

As you may remember from chapter 1, it was during one of those international layovers I discovered Sylvia Browne's book, an experience that was a crucial turning point for me. The information about practical spirituality and loving yourself wasn't new to me at that time. I had been previously introduced to it by a wonderful lady in Belgium. However, Ms. Browne's material certainly came to me at the right time to refresh my understanding of it all.

When I say "right time," I mean that quite literally. This wonderful book reminded me about the purpose of life and the evolution of the soul. It contained a wealth of information on how to better deal with life's challenges and how to speak up for oneself. As I was devouring the fascinating concepts in the book, little did I know that the Universe was helping me prepare for the next dramatic event in my life. A few short weeks later, Sabena declared bankruptcy.

This was extraordinary. Belgium was in a state of shock. Demonstrations took place everywhere. Employees from different departments of the airline came together and took to the streets with banners to demand the Belgian government step in and save Sabena. It was all to no avail.

Of course it wasn't a happy experience for me, but by this time I had grown spiritually, and I felt a lot stronger inside. I didn't take part in any of the protests. In fact, on the day of the actual bankruptcy, there was a photograph of me in the national newspaper serving champagne onboard a plane with a huge smile on my face!

I was crew on the last Sabena flight from Nice to Brussels, and I was determined to make it a good experience for everyone onboard, including myself. I refused to jump on the bandwagon of bitterness and self-pity. Reaping the first major benefit from walking the path of practical spirituality, I was able to zoom out and accept the bigger picture. I was given yet another opportunity to grow.

Like most other people, I had no idea what to do next. What I did know, however, was that this was a door opening, not closing. I felt blessed because I had time to explore my future, and my body had the opportunity to recuperate from accumulated jetlag. Suddenly there was so much free time. I went out a lot with my friends, making up for lost time. My job with Sabena had taken me away frequently, and I had worked all hours of the day and night, including weekends and holidays. I had had to miss out on many parties and nights out with my friends, so it felt great to be part of the group again. I certainly enjoyed all the attention. My friends respected that I had been made redundant and it felt like I had been given the right to party all night!

But after a couple of months it was time to focus on my career again. In all honesty, I knew deep inside I didn't really want to go back to flying. However, helping people was still as close as I had come to discovering the purpose to my life, so I applied for another job as cabin crew, this time abroad.

The ad on the Internet sounded great–working for the national airline of Japan as part of their London-based European crew. Wow! The prospect of moving to London was big. Huge. It certainly garnered me even more attention from the friends around me. London was calling, and my future was looking brighter and brighter.

However, when I was offered the job and left Belgium and everyone I knew behind me, I didn't realize I was about to be reminded of what loneliness feels like. I felt absolutely dreadful during my first couple of weeks in London, a vibrant city that is home to millions of people. I went from being the center of attention to nobody paying me any attention at all. For some bizarre reason, I had imagined I would be picked up from the airport by my lovely host family where I would stay during my crew training. It was an illusion. There was no host family. Like most people who leave their native countries to move abroad, I had to take care of everything myself—a place to live, bank accounts, transport, credit card, cell phone, medical insurance. And I had to do it in English, a language in which I wasn't comfortable.

This experience was another steep learning curve for me, and it took all of my energy and faith to make it. Thank heavens I can be stubborn and perhaps even prideful sometimes. I would have given anything to go back to my friends in Belgium, but I wasn't going to admit I wasn't happy. So I stayed in London.

After the initial grueling months, things smoothed out. I made new friends, grew more fluent with the language, and began to feel a bit more settled in the UK. Granted, I was fully aware that my passion for being airline crew was fading fast, but working with my Japanese colleagues was a worthwhile experience. And I enjoyed visiting exciting new places as far away as Sydney and Delhi.

Throughout this transitional phase of my life, I was able to draw strength from my spiritual beliefs. Once more practical spirituality was my comforter and my compass, guiding me through this adventure. I realized my soul longed to have all these valuable experiences, and that motivated me to hang on. Experiencing extreme loneliness, adjusting to the very different cultures of the UK and Japan, being forced to grow up quickly —apparently they were all items on my soul's wish list!

A Thank You and Final Goodbye to the Dark

I would like to thank you for taking this journey with me through some of the significant events and turning points in my life. I can say, hand on heart, that I've processed the traumas and fully see these experiences for what they were—a critical part of my spiritual growth. I am very clear about why these events occurred in my life. That said, I can't say that revisiting these memories has been particularly relaxing and enjoyable. So I am taking the opportunity here and now to say a final goodbye to everything that happened.

We all have challenges to deal with on our path to happiness, and every one of us is in search of emotional and spiritual healing. Rather than suffer in a dark and lonely corner of our mind, we can look at how others have managed to navigate through their hard times.

With this chapter I wanted to open my heart to you and show you how I navigated (and continue to navigate for that matter) my hard times. Whatever unfolds before me, I know and trust that everything is a piece of my life's puzzle and shows up with perfect divine timing. I am aware that any experience—good or bad, easy or hard—contributes to my growth as a person and to the evolution of my soul.

There are learning opportunities everywhere. We can try to escape them, or we can turn toward them with open arms. I know turning toward them and accepting them is far easier said than done. However, I also know that unbeatable feeling of satisfaction that lifts us up when we make it through the experience and come out the other end. We look back and think, "Wow, I have truly come a long way."

One Final Thought

I would like to leave you with one final thought. I believe we should always be very careful when we voice an opinion about someone who is or has been a victim of anything—sexual abuse, bullying, a life-threatening illness, a car accident, a natural disaster, domestic violence—to name just a few. A misinterpretation of the spiritual laws of cocreation and attraction can lead us to jump to the conclusion that someone created or attracted this experience and is therefore somehow less worthy or flawed.

Actually quite the opposite is true. Once we understand that becoming a victim is an experience the soul has sought in order to evolve, we can suspend judgment and blame and move toward compassion. When that person goes on to make profound changes in their life and transcend victimhood, we are observing a spiritual growth worthy of our acknowledgment and respect.

Those of you who have suffered victimizing experiences may feel inspired to assist others on their journeys because you understand what they are going through. You may become the pathfinder who helps them find the way to a lighter life. I know my personal knowledge of pain, loneliness, and abuse makes me a better coach and supports my spiritual work.

Summary of This Chapter

- Everything that's ever happened to me, no matter how difficult, has served my soul's purpose, and I am truly grateful for that. The growth process is the same for all of us. The sooner we accept the value inherent in this growth, the quicker we can move on with life.
- Think of a very difficult time in your life. What meaning could you give to the events you experienced? What might have been the learning opportunity? Can you see how everything has helped your soul to evolve?

Feeling on top of the world sometimes requires experiencing rock bottom first.

CHAPTER 4

Freedom from Emotional Baggage

Life truly is a grand *opportunity*.

I believe that life is a journey chosen by our soul to experience not only life itself but also all of the emotions associated with the trials of life such as divorce, illness, job loss, financial stress, losing a loved one, and so forth.

The soul decides to experience life on Earth on its own accord. Incarnating is not something a soul is forced to do. It is a voluntary decision. And that decision was made for a very good reason. Because the soul is a part of the Universal God Source, it may contain infinite wisdom, but it longs to experience life in order to practice that wisdom. That is why life is a grand opportunity for our soul, because it enables the soul to apply its wisdom in a practical way. This practical application of its wisdom is a vital part of the soul's evolution and journey toward wholeness. Wholeness is achieved when the soul has finished journeying through different incarnations and returns to the Universal God Source forever.

Depending on its desired learning outcomes, the soul then chooses a certain outline for this lifetime (i.e., family, geographical location, career, etc.). For example, if a soul wants to experience solitude, it may choose to take on a life as a Zen monk in Tibet. Or perhaps a soul wishes to experience poverty and therefore incarnates in a slum in a poor country. Should it wish to undergo mistreatment by a family member, a soul might incarnate in a family where another soul will facilitate that experience as part of both their learning outcomes. When the journey is completed, the soul detaches from the body and returns to the astral world. Depending on its evolutionary stage, this is either where the soul resides until its next incarnation or where it returns to remain with the Universal God Source.

I'm reminded of a client who asked me if our soul is somehow trapped inside our body until we depart this life. She was worried her soul was imprisoned by her physical body and was longing to go back to the Other Side. I assured her our soul is here by free will, thus fully enjoying the journey on Earth and it determines its own destiny. The soul is far more powerful than our physical body. It is a form of energy and is, in fact, everywhere. It is omnipresent. Our body is but one location to which it's currently attached. You could say the soul has one foot in our physical body and one foot in the astral plane, where it continues to store the experiences it gains through the accumulation of lifetimes.

But the growth of a soul doesn't just happen by undergoing the big events in life. It also happens because of the many aspects of our personalities with which it needs to contend. Feelings and character traits such as perfectionism, guilt, anger, self-doubt, and jealousy—to name just a few—offer tremendous opportunities for growth.

The big events of our lives come and go and often seriously knock us off balance for a while. However, it's the devils within that can create the greatest havoc in our lives because they never seem to go away! For example, a good friend of mine has a wonderful life filled with luxury, yet she is such a worrier. She worries about what others think of her, she worries about losing her fortune, and, if there's nothing to worry about, she worries about that too! She's a master at creating something to worry about out of thin air.

It's been my experience that overcoming those personal traits can be the biggest challenge of them all. "It's not the mountain we conquer—but ourselves," Sir Edmund Hillary once said. I love that quote. Indeed, there are some excellent opportunities for personal growth and advancement to a higher level of spirituality when we learn to let go of emotional baggage.

Imagine the harmony we can bring back into our lives and what truly happy people we can become if we let go of guilt, overcome our jealousy, stop blaming others, build better relationships with our families, and release our fears, etc. That's wonderful progress for the soul; that's when we have seized the opportunity to transform ourselves into lighter beings. That's when we become stronger, more grounded, more authentic, and thus better friends to ourselves and to others.

In this chapter, I will go over some of those daily issues and aspects of our personalities that prevent us from feeling lighter and freer. You will learn how to conquer those issues and create daily happiness instead. I chose the issues and aspects that trouble my clients the most because I suspect they trouble you the most as well.

If we want to create a life of a lifetime, it's useful to focus on what we can do on a daily basis to help us with that. The funny thing about this luxury item called inner happiness is that it's totally free and available in abundance. We often think that something incredible needs to happen in order to manifest joy, harmony, and inner peace. That's not true. If we learn how to make it through each day in a meaningful way, daily happiness will flow as a result.

Not every day will be a walk in the park, but it *will* be valuable for the evolution of your soul nonetheless. That's very important to remember because your soul evolves always and in many ways. One bad day, month, or even year shouldn't bring you down or catapult you back into negative thinking and old habits that no longer serve you. You need to maintain your balance and focus on your desire to live with integrity. You can make a commitment to yourself *today* to start over. That's how you create the canvas upon which the Universe can paint positive experiences.

A man named Michael approached me one evening after one of my lectures on personal development. He was fascinated by the concept of loving and appreciating oneself. He wanted to talk to me in person because he wasn't quite sure if it was really okay for him to love himself. Michael was genuinely concerned that self-love meant becoming selfish and obnoxious.

I told him he was exactly right.

I explained that, if he feared the path of self-development would lead him into a world of egoism and narcissism, there was a real chance that would indeed happen if he wasn't careful. Of course Michael wasn't expecting this kind of reply, but he understood the point I was making. Often our fearful thoughts stop us from moving forward in life. Sometimes they even help create that which we fear the most! I'm happy to report that Michael changed his perspective and embraced self-love.

Changing perspectives was another big part of my lecture that evening. It is also one of my favorite coaching tools because it is so useful. When you change the way you look at a situation, the situation becomes more manageable.

I went on to suggest to Michael that loving himself wasn't selfish, but that not loving himself *was*. This was a moment of awakening for Michael. He felt relieved and made the commitment to work on letting go his old beliefs. From now on, he intended to focus on applying the self-improvement principles I had talked about that evening.

When I noted that having a positive, yet realistic attitude toward creating a better life would help him to attract precisely that, Michael agreed. And it certainly turned out to be the case for him. Michael sends me regular updates on how his life is flourishing now. He has learned to appreciate his own company without being selfish and has become so fascinated by personal development he recently enrolled in life coaching training so he can help other people change *their* perspectives.

Your personal and spiritual growth accelerates when you look inside and contemplate your needs and desires. It's okay for you to pursue a lighter life. You are allowed to love and appreciate yourself and to explore new ways to help you do that. That's not being selfish; that's respecting yourself. And respecting yourself is not just beneficial for your mind and body, it's necessary. Remember that you, both in all your glory *and* in all your negative thinking, are still a spark of the Universal God Source. Embrace the idea that you can work on yourself and change aspects of your personality without becoming self-absorbed or a tyrant.

Now is a good time to rise above the dark, heavy clouds of low self-esteem and fears. Now is a good time to reclaim your self-worth and create inner peace. And now is a good time to feel lighter and restore harmony in your life by gracefully letting go of emotional baggage. Here's where to start.

Guilt

Letting go of guilt is difficult for many people. That's especially the case for those with a sensitive personality who want to help and do good. Since most people who are interested in practical spirituality belong in this category, I want to cover this topic in detail. After all, this chapter is about dropping emotional baggage, and guilt is probably the heaviest burden of all. Guilt is always present and very hard to block out. It's the weight on your shoulders, the voice whispering in your ear, "You don't deserve to be happy because you did this or that."

Silencing that voice can be difficult. In many ways, guilt has become your life companion—a nasty acquaintance you would be better off without. Oddly, when you look around, you'll see many people who don't have a clue what guilt feels like. That doesn't mean they are saints. They just don't make feeling guilty a priority in their lives. And some of those people who are seemingly impervious to feeling guilty may not make having a clear conscience a priority either. And that's the difference between them and you. You do value a clear conscience. You are ready to meet a more authentic version of yourself. In order to do this, you need to work through your guilt so you can release it for good.

I felt guilty for many years. It was just awful, and at times I was paralyzed by shame. I was convinced I was a bad person because I had abused someone's trust by taking something that didn't belong to me. Because of that action, I believed the doors to a happy life were forever closed to me.

At the time, I wasn't too sure if God existed, but if He did, surely He would never forgive me. At least that's what I thought. Years later, after my moment of awakening in Boston and after learning about practical spirituality, I finally gathered enough courage to do what I teach people today to do. I took responsibility for my actions.

One day I arranged to sit down with the person from whom I had taken something. Surprisingly, I felt calm and in control. I was mentally prepared to take the blow I felt I deserved. Assisted by the Universe that day, the energy of truth filled every cell in me and gave me the courage I needed. I explained what I had done and that I wanted to rectify the situation. I offered to do whatever it would take to make things right. The meeting went well, and I was blessed with being forgiven for my actions. The relief that brought me was amazing.

To this day, I believe that things worked out the way they did because I was determined to take responsibility, to shed my burden, and to get on with my life no matter what the consequences. Anything would be better than that awful feeling of guilt! I would do whatever I had to do to release the guilt, and I did. What a wonderful feeling! Now I could finally move on, truly feeling lighter and more mature.

Just apologizing for something you've done wrong without the slightest intention of being serious about it doesn't work. It's a waste of time and energy for everyone involved, including you. That's not what I'm talking about here. If you want to make things right, you've got to come from a place of honesty and integrity. You've got to want to be able to look at yourself in the mirror at two o'clock in the morning and not turn away. The more honest and authentic you are when you make your amends, the more likely things will work out and be settled for good.

Please don't worry about God waiting in the clouds to punish you. Unfortunately that's religious dogma used to instill fear in people. It's also a pretty clever tool for exercising control. If anything, don't you think God would rather you worked through your guilt issues instead of sitting on your backside, scared, doing nothing about it? You are a part of the Universal God Source, so the only deity you report to is yourself. No matter what you may have done wrong, you can choose today to clear your conscience and flow into long overdue emotional freedom.

I would also like to address another kind of guilt many people needlessly suffer from—the terrible *Shoulds and Coulds*. As if our lives aren't already busy enough, many of us use a lot of energy excessively worrying about how we *should* have done things differently, how we *could* have done things differently. Those *Shoulds and Coulds* gnaw away at our conscience like nasty little termites.

Here's what to do the next time you feel an attack of the *Shoulds and Coulds* coming on. Ask yourself if it was your intention to create this particular outcome you are upset about. If your answer is a firm no (and chances are this will be the case 99 percent of the time), then doesn't your guilt seem rather foolish? If it wasn't your intention to hurt someone or cause trouble, then please just let it go. Letting go takes some practice, but I learned to do it, and so can you. It's a very efficient and self-respectful way of clearing your head and gaining a fresh perspective.

Here are some of the most common phrases I hear that are a tip-off to me that unnecessary guilt is at work. "I could have done more." "I should have made a better decision." "I could have tried harder." "I shouldn't have said this or that." The list goes on and on and on. The constant worry that results from a bad case of the *Shoulds* and *Coulds* is a colossal waste of valuable time. It creates a self-inflicted energy that drains you and leaves you feeling weak and stuck. If you are inflicting that kind of worry on yourself, please realize that the only one who is suffering is you.

Pay careful attention to whom you surround yourself with. Your sensitive nature might make it too easy for people to inflict pain and guilt upon you. If you know this is the case for you, rest assured that there's no time like the present to break this pattern. You are a soul having an experience of life by taking on human form. That in itself is an incredible achievement. I encourage you to be proud of who and what you are. Your journey here is far too precious to let people take advantage of your sensitive nature. Remember that you teach people how to treat you.

Anger

Dreaming of daily happiness when you're carrying anger around inside isn't going to work out very well. Whether you're a calm person, rather volatile, or a bit of a drama queen, we all get angry sometimes. It's okay. It happens to everyone. And since it is going to happen to you, then let's figure out how you can deal with your anger appropriately instead of being rushed to the nearest mental institute in a straitjacket. Sometimes all you need to do to release your anger appropriately is to really understand what exactly triggered it and why you reacted so strongly. Anger can be a very helpful signpost pointing to something we need to pay attention to or change. And sometimes anger is an obstacle on the pathway to happiness. If it's simmering away on a low boil, we may not even be aware of it even though it is holding us prisoner. When we are pushed too far, it erupts like a volcano and brings out the worst in us. We say or do things we regret.

Now is a good time to look your anger in the eyes and release it. In my coaching work, I see three main causes for anger—other people, ourselves, and situations. Here are a few simple and effective three-step approaches to help you deal with each of these causes.

Angry with someone?

Face it, frame it, and forget about it

So. . . someone has upset you. It can hurt. It's frustrating. The good news? The quicker you acknowledge someone has caused you pain, the sooner you can take action to eradicate that pain. Don't be too proud to admit to yourself that you were knocked off balance. Pretending to be untouchable is a lot harder than just allowing yourself to be vulnerable. In other words, face it. Face that you are angry, accept it, own it. Whether someone has said nasty things about you, taken advantage of your generosity, betrayed your trust, used your belongings without your permission, or just plain annoyed the heck out of you, face what has happened and your reaction to it. Allow yourself to be angry. You may be a sensitive and spiritual person, but that doesn't mean you're not allowed to get angry.

The next step is something I find very helpful—frame your anger. Give it meaning. That meaning will be different for each of us since we each have different learning opportunities in life. What can you learn about yourself when you're angry with someone? How do you benefit from feeling angry? Do you feel it serves you? What can you learn from your reactions? Whatever your answers, once you recognize your anger as part of who you are and a tool for self-discovery, you will understand your anger more easily and release it more quickly.

There is always spiritual value in dealing with your anger. Perhaps you needed the anger from a particular confrontation to help you learn how to speak up for yourself. Or perhaps your soul yearned for the opportunity to get angry with someone and then learn how to forgive. Souls often decide to help each other evolve, and of course Planet Earth is a great place to do exactly that. The souls involved will mutually agree upon a scenario where everyone can learn a valuable lesson about anger—not because we have to learn lessons but because our souls want to experience the growth only anger can provide.

I recently met with my coaching client, Roger. When I first saw him, he seemed strong and self-confident. But as I started to tune into him, I sensed a lot of suppressed emotion, and I soon realized that he was in a vulnerable state.

"I am so angry with my friends," Roger declared. Not one of them has even bothered to phone me to see how I was coping!"

Roger, who lived in the United States, had recently lost both his mother and his beloved uncle within a very short space of time, and he was back in the UK for their funerals. Although he could come to terms with their passing after their long illnesses, Roger was clearly upset about the lack of support from his friends back home.

"I've had no support whatsoever!" Roger told me.

"I can imagine how hard it must have been for you," I replied. "But look how well you have dealt with everything, and all by yourself," I added. "You handled it well because you are a very strong person."

"I know I'm strong!" he snapped. "That's the whole problem. I'm never allowed to be weak. I'm always on the barricades for everyone else, but when I need help, nobody is there for me!"

Roger broke down in tears. He didn't understand why he had reacted like this, since he is usually very much in control of his emotions. I reassured him it was perfectly okay for him to cry. He felt abandoned by his best friends—those same friends who looked up to him and admired what he had achieved in life. I gave Roger time to really grab his anger by the horns and allow himself to really feel his pain. For Roger, facing the pain meant admitting that he was indeed in pain.

I told Roger how I had learned to frame my anger. I remember the look on his face, as if to say, "What on earth do you mean?" Probably all he wanted from his session with me was a listening ear and some comforting words. But for the first time ever someone was going to tell him about how to frame his anger.

I invited Roger to take a small step back—to zoom out just a bit—to see if there was something he could learn from there. At first he was resistant. "I've learned that my friends are not who I thought they were, that's for sure," he sighed.

I empathized with him, but I felt it was time to give him something to think about that would help him frame his anger so he could discover a different perspective on the situation. I suggested that sometimes people don't quite know how to be there for us when we need it most. As strange as it may sound, this can be especially true for our best friends. It doesn't mean they don't want to help us. They simply may not know how.

Roger was surprised.

"In addition," I continued, "You are always the strong one in your friends' eyes. So there's a very good chance they were quite simply afraid to help. They were afraid to say the wrong thing, or perhaps they feared your reaction. The last thing they wanted to do was upset you even more."

I had taken a gamble by telling him this, but it's my experience that strong-willed clients generally appreciate a more direct approach. Roger was no different, and my gamble paid off. He immediately understood the bigger picture. He could see how he had been worrying over nothing and had wasted a lot of energy doing so. This proved to be a valuable learning opportunity for him. He realized the often hidden consequences of being a strong man. He also learned to trust his friends more and give them the time and space to be there for him in ways that worked for *them*.

I suggested Roger phone his friends. Two days later, he called to say he had had some of his best chats ever with them. They were all relieved to hear from him. He told me his friends had known he was going through a very hard time, but none of them had thought they were *good enough* to be able to help him. They were convinced they wouldn't find the right words. They all thought he would be his usual strong self and handle the situation his way. Roger could now begin to let go of his anger at his friends much more easily and flow into emotional freedom once again.

The topic of being angry with people is often on the agenda during coaching sessions. There is no doubt that sometimes people get seriously on our nerves! Even the calmest of us loses our balance once in a while. Isn't there a passage in the Bible where even Jesus gets angry at the merchants for carrying out business in the temple? Anger happens—to all of us. The key is to face it as soon as possible, frame it (what's the lesson?), let it go, and move on.

Holding on to your anger doesn't serve you. Resentment and especially revenge are poisons that attack you from within. Focus on what a good person *you* are. Admire yourself for not staying angry for long. People can hurt you only when you let them by giving away your power. The sooner you pick yourself up when someone has upset you, the sooner you can move on.

Angry at yourself?

Face it, frame it, and forgive yourself

Whatever you might have done (or didn't do) and hate yourself for it—now is a good time to let it go. Being angry at yourself, which can sometimes turn into self-hatred, is a very destructive energy. Constantly beating yourself up can be very dangerous for both your emotional and physical well-being. It is not uncommon for different types of diseases to manifest as a result of unprocessed anger aimed at oneself.

Think of something you punish yourself for—something you think you should have done differently, an opportunity you shouldn't have let slip through your hands. Anything goes, even if you have more than one issue. Use this moment to face your inner anger at yourself. Are you willing to let it go? To accept the learning opportunity and then move on?

Remember what an incredible divine being you really are. You are a soul on a journey, evolving and growing every minute of every day, gaining valuable life experience from everything that goes on in your life. Yes, that's right. *Everything.* If you wish to grow spiritually, accept whatever you hate yourself for. Accept it as a part of your journey.

Your life is a puzzle that wouldn't be complete without this particular piece. It may not be the most beautiful piece, but it's a piece nonetheless. Once you have managed to do this—to frame your anger—I encourage you to forgive yourself. No one else needs to forgive you—just you.

The Universal God Source already sees you as perfect, so forgiveness won't matter when you arrive at the end of this lifetime. It shouldn't concern you, since there's nothing you need to be forgiven for. Your life is a collection of experiences—happy or sad. They all contribute to who you are. Once you can accept that once in a while you might make a mistake and that it is inherent to your human incarnation, you'll see that your inner anger has become redundant.

You can decide right here and right now to let go of this burden. The past is behind you, and the future can be better if you allow it to be. Forgive yourself. Perhaps next time you can make a more informed decision or do things differently so you attract a different outcome.

Angry at a situation?

Face it, frame it, and refocus

Sometimes we get angry at events that are beyond our direct control—environmental damage, traffic congestion, disasters, public transport, inflation, political unrest, injustice, violence, or simply the local gym club raising membership fees yet again. Whether it's on our doorstep or on the other side of the Earth, certain things can really make our blood boil. This anger we feel inside is often caused by fear and disappointment—for example, the fear we feel when we look at the destruction of the Earth's rainforest or the disappointment we feel at the poor decisions made for us by our political leaders.

Face whatever is upsetting you, but make sure your own world doesn't stop turning. Don't let it affect you too much. I'm not saying don't care. What I mean is you shouldn't allow situations that concern you to consume you. If all you do is worry yourself sick, then that's certainly not going to heal your anger or the situation. Instead, frame the anger you experience by expanding the horizons of your thinking and by changing your attitude toward these issues.

Disasters and accidents don't just happen. They occur on people's paths for reasons we can't always accept with our rational minds. But it all makes sense on a soul level. No matter how unfortunate it may seem, there's always a reason why certain people are involved in certain difficult situations at a certain time. This doesn't mean you need to stop caring, but you do need to find a way to get past the shock of what happens, drop the drama, and focus on how you can make a difference, no matter how large or small. How about organizing a charity event to raise money to help those affected by a natural disaster? Can you approach a children's hospital and offer to do some volunteer work? You get the idea.

The bottom line is this. Whatever the situation that triggers your anger may be, whatever makes you fearful or disillusioned, rather than feeling sorry for someone (or for yourself), refocus on the way forward by taking the situation in stride. At the same time, develop your compassion, patience, and acceptance on your path of personal and spiritual growth.

A dear friend of mine and her family were away from home for the Christmas holidays. They were riding in a taxi on Christmas day when they were hit by a van that failed to give way. Joy's son and daughter were badly bruised, but it was her husband who suffered the worst injuries. He was hospitalized with compacted vertebrae and cracked ribs. Joy had three cracked ribs herself, and her back muscles were in spasm.

The day after the accident, things got even worse when Joy's neighbor called with bad news. The pipe to Joy's boiler had burst in the ceiling between the kitchen and dining room, and the ceiling had come down. Hot water had gone everywhere, the living room carpet was soaked, and the kitchen and all the floors and furniture were ruined.

When I spoke to Joy about her ordeal, she said, "Everything happens for a reason, even the bad things. I don't blame anyone. Blame only holds you back. The driver of the van ruined my Christmas, but my heart goes out to him because he didn't mean to hurt anyone. He was just careless. So he carries no blame in my eyes. And as for our house, well, that was one gigantic learning curve. But I believe it happened to help me understand a thing or two about patience, acceptance, and remaining calm."

Jealousy and Envy

I don't know how many people are prepared to admit it, but I do know that many people suffer from being jealous or envious. And suffering it is. You only have to look at what they say or what they do to know this is true.

I would rather run a marathon in the Sahara Desert than endure jealousy ever again. I used to be quite jealous when I was a teenager. And as I'm writing this, I can recall just how horrible it felt to be jealous. It's a weird, nasty energy that overpowers you, making you say or do things you never would usually.

Looking back, I suppose I was bound to be jealous. With everything going on, from growing up in the shadow of my superstar brother to the bullying and all the rest of it, I can clearly see why I had jealous thoughts regularly. The world was passing me by or so I thought, and I was trapped inside a cage of low self-esteem and desperation.

I probably shouldn't be too hard on myself since I was only a teenager after all, and a rather unhappy one at that. However, despite the lack of positive love and attention given to me, I was the one who had allowed myself to crawl into that cage in the first place. I was the one who had created the jealousy monster.

If you suffer from jealousy or envy, could it be you have created this cage for yourself? Could it be you are the one who has created the monster? I'm not saying this to upset you, but rather to help you see how you have become a victim of being a victim. Jealousy and envy almost always originate from a lack of attention in one form or another. Not only are you deprived of this attention (love, friendship, material goods, etc.), but you make things worse for yourself by consciously suffering from this lack. You behave in ways you know very well are not appropriate, but you do so almost as a defense mechanism.

For example, let's presume your friend has something you're jealous of—a brand new car, a job promotion, a boyfriend. It's not important who or what it is. What *is* important is you end up saying something that leads to an argument and, before you know it, you've alienated yet another friend. You deeply regret what you said. Maybe you even hate yourself for it. But you don't know what to do about it or, more importantly, how to stop it from happening again.

And then, in a moment of magic and at a time that's perfect for your own personal development, practical spirituality crosses your path. And it offers you the solution to overcome your jealousy and envy. Granted, it will take a change in your attitude, and any change in attitude may take a little bit of work. But at least practical spirituality offers you the unconditional freedom to try. Whereas most religions might say "You should," practical spirituality says, "You might want to try to." The spiritual path reconnects you to your own power and encourages you to discover your own truths.

That's why it has been and still is so helpful to me. It taught me I was worthy and it was never too late to make positive changes in my life. The more I found out about the value of acknowledging my self-worth, the more I started applying this wonderful concept in my daily routine, and the transformation happened quickly.

As I began to really appreciate myself and accept that I was empowered to create my own emotional heaven or hell, my jealous attitude melted away like snow in the sun. And with it went the self-hatred and depression it caused. At last I could see that being jealous was an adverse reaction to the lack of attention and appreciation in my life. As I began to love and accept myself more, that void was soon filled with genuine, healthy self-respect. I no longer needed to be jealous because whatever I might have been jealous about I could now provide for myself.

The great thing about my personal renaissance was people started to notice the changes in me. They felt attracted to come and talk to me, whereas before they might have been pushed away by my aura of depression. I had become a much calmer person, was enjoying a long overdue sense of inner peace, and radiated contentment.

These days, if I meet a fellow coach or author who has accomplished something amazing, rather than being envious, I fully admire their achievement. Then I simply go about my business and see if I can find inspiration from this encounter. That way I can take any potential envy and turn it into positive energy that motivates me.

So, if you recognize yourself even a little bit in what I've described, you may want to address whatever is missing in your life that makes you jealous of other people. Like a butterfly shedding the cocoon it no longer needs, you too can let go of the suffocating jealousy that imprisons you. Any envy you have of someone else's success will only slow down your own. It's as simple as that. You have your own wonderful personality, your own soul's agenda, and your own innate skills and talents. You possess more than enough resources to attain contentment. You are always and continually loved by a nonjudgmental Universal God Source. I invite you now to love yourself, reflect on your magnificence, and enjoy the inner peace that is your birthright.

What if your family members or friends or colleagues behave jealously toward you and make your life difficult? This can be a source of significant frustration, especially when you didn't do anything to provoke their jealousy. It is wise to approach this issue with sensitivity. Easier said than done, I know, and your patience will be tested. But there's a gift for you in all this. The opportunities for your personal growth are plentiful.

Let's say you've achieved something remarkable—maybe you've earned an additional diploma or you've lost a lot of weight. Your friend makes a sharp remark that hurts you. She didn't mean to come across that way or to hurt you, but she is feeling envious. She's disappointed with herself for not following through on her own ambitions.

So when you come along, excited to share your achievement with her, she says the wrong thing at the wrong time. That's all. If you know her intention isn't to be nasty or mean, then be smart enough (and willing enough) to let it go. It would be a shame to fall out over a single unfortunate remark that was never aimed directly at you in the first place.

When I find myself in a similar situation, I stay calm and may even say a few words of encouragement. "You can do this or that too, you know," or "Would you like to see a similar result for yourself?" I've discovered that people soon calm down and usually realize their comment was misplaced.

However, sometimes a situation can be more serious. If you are sub-jected to continuous jealous behavior that's starting to affect your emotional well-being, it's time to act. Let's face it. Some people really don't know how to deal with their jealousy, and it can make your life very difficult.

Whatever you do, they try to top it. Whatever you say, they ridicule it. Whatever you accomplish, they criticize it. And on it goes. After having advanced your soul by demonstrating patience, you now have an additional opportunity for growth—by refusing to be a victim of such poor behavior. No matter who it is—lover, friend, relative, colleague—it is time to speak up for yourself and make it clear you will no longer tolerate their behavior.

However, never give someone a piece of your mind in public. Take the person to one side and make sure you know what you're going to say. Tell them what you have noticed and how it affects you and your relationship with them. Let them know why you feel there is no need for jealousy on their part. Bear in mind that, no matter what their reaction, it's going to be a spiritual opportunity for growth for that person too.

You may need to put a brave face on, but ultimately there's spiritual value in this confrontation for both parties. Be yourself, be resilient, and know that if they take it the wrong way, then that's their choice. And remember never to feel guilty about anything as long as you don't hurt someone intentionally. And since you have no wish to hurt anyone but are just getting your point across, then there's nothing for you to worry about, I promise.

If—and it's an unlikely if—the person decides not to talk to you any-more, then that's probably a good thing. It may not be comfortable at first, but it may well bring the peace you need after having been subjected to their jealousy for so long. Welcome this breathing space and, before you know it, new friends will move into the energetic space you have cleared for them.

Fear of Loneliness/The Need to Belong/ Recognition/Finding Love

Even though I love to write and could write an entire book about any of these topics separately because they are such significant issues for most people, I will address them together in this section because they are very much related.

Most of us choose to be with a partner so that we may feel safe and avoid feeling lonely. I think it's also fair to say that we all want to be recognized to some extent for our actions and that this recognition is one form of love exhibited between partners. Also, we all like to belong, to be a part of a group in one way or another—whether it's being a member of a hobby club, a business partner, an affiliate of a federation, a member of a church group, or working as part of an office team. We have only to look at the astounding success of social networking websites to know that human beings have a need to belong.

But what about those who say they can quite happily live on an island on their own? I think if they tried it, they would find that wasn't so. In fact, making such a statement is a way of getting the attention they so adamantly claim not to need. So I think it's safe to say that we all like to belong, be loved, and be recognized.

Have you ever wondered where this need originates? A need that is so strong we do all kinds of crazy things just to satisfy it? (Think about your last brush with unrequited love.) Let's put our spiritually tinted glasses on and take a closer look.

Like a child going to school for the first time and spending an entire day away from his mother or like a young bird leaving the safety of the nest to take to the sky, our soul experiences the same heartache and fear and requires the same courage to temporarily leave the Universal God Source to embark on a new physical reincarnation. The soul's decision to journey on its own for a period of time creates a void, a "soul ache."

You could compare it to being away from your family when you go on a trip abroad. You might be away from your loved ones and be homesick once in a while, but you're still connected to and a member of your family. Although the soul is never completely disconnected from the Universal God Source, it certainly is on a "trip abroad" when it incarnates here on Earth.

Depending on the level of spiritual awareness the soul chooses for its human incarnation, some people will better understand where this soul ache comes from than others. Having this awareness, which you can deepen by engaging in practical spirituality, is a tremendous source of support to you, especially in times of great loneliness and despair.

Are you wondering how exactly you benefit from knowing you're a soul on a journey? Especially when sometimes you feel so alone, so different from other people? Because the knowledge of who you really are offers an explanation, gives you a reason for what can feel like an overwhelming desire for love, affection, belonging, and recognition. And when you know why you have these strong emotions, you can handle them better. You can make your emotions work for you instead of against you. You can maintain your dignity by no longer making desperate attempts to be loved and recognized.

For me, discovering this was pure magic! As I learned about the journey of my soul, I gained new perspectives on all aspects of my life. I became aware of my connection to the Universal God Source and that I was much more than I thought I was. Of course I have experienced heartache and various challenges since then, but I've been able to cope much better. Aaah . . . those wonderful, practical benefits of walking the spiritual path! Knowing that I'm here on a temporary basis really makes me want to get the most from this experience and gives me unparalleled amounts of strength. My energy levels are forever fueled by the knowledge that there's a purpose behind my incarnation.

Do you worry about still being single? Do you somehow feel like you're not making a difference in the world? Take heart. Know you are *never* on your own. Yes, I know it may feel that way and feeling that way can be awful (at best). But your loneliness will ease when you remind yourself that you are never truly alone. Your soul is forever connected to the Universal God Source. The loneliness you experience, whether it is short or long term, is actually the result of being temporarily away from that Source. If you will remember your soul's loneliness that you feel so deeply is a natural and normal part of being a human spiritual being here on Earth, you will find your longing will ease.

Besides, you are not quite as alone as you might think. There's a whole team of spiritual guides and helpers who are always looking over your shoulder. These are spiritual connections you made prior to embarking on your journey. I will be talking about spiritual helpers later on. For now, simply be open to the idea that you are always surrounded by spiritual energies, and it too will help alleviate your loneliness.

And you *are* making a difference in this world. I promise you that there's no need to panic about this whatsoever. Through all of your actions and engagements with others, you are shining your light, probably much more than you know. Whether it's a simple smile to an elderly person or founding your own business that creates jobs for hundreds of people, both are equally important each in their own way.

If you don't like your current situation, change it. There is always something you can do. Join a local sports club, write about your interests on a web blog, start a hobby group, or phone an old friend for a long overdue chat. Give the Universe a sign that you are ready to meet people and ready to shine even brighter. With a little willingness from your end, a change in attitude is bound to bring about a change in your circumstances.

Perfectionism

I think the term "perfectionism" is often misunderstood and therefore misused. It sounds very negative, conjuring up images of people being slaves to their own unreasonably high standards. Perfectionism is a form of stress, but stress can be a good thing. It's a tool—a compass—telling you whether you're flowing or struggling. Let's explore how you can use stress sensibly as a wonderful addition to your self-empowerment tool kit.

If you get stressed about something, it can mean you're not projecting your energy in a useful way. But when you use stress as a motivational energy, it can be very helpful to you. It's the same with perfectionism. It doesn't have to be a curse. The next time you are frantically trying to accomplish something, all you need to do is to be aware of what's happening. Remember the framing principle when we talked about anger? It's exactly the same with perfectionism. When you realize you're taking too much on or you're constantly pushing yourself too hard, take a step back and be gentle with yourself. If you don't slow down and take stock once in a while, you'll become exhausted. You can experience burnout, and that prevents you from achieving anything at all.

Wanting to do things well is a blessing. However, doing so to impress yourself or others is when it becomes foolish. That's when perfectionism turns into a heavy burden. If you get too invested in what somebody else thinks about you, you give away your power. As with many daily issues, your attitude will make the difference. If you're inspired by the task ahead of you, by all means go for it, but use your energy wisely and pace yourself.

Today's society expects us to produce nonstop results, but you can't be a slave to that rhythm or you'll go crazy. Find a way to balance your time and energy. (If you need help with that, approach a life coach or support group. Simply do a quick search on the Internet or check out the directory section in the back of a lifestyle magazine.) When you learn to befriend your perfectionism, it becomes a blessing rather than an obstacle on your path to daily happiness.

My mother has been a primary school teacher for three decades. She has always been a perfectionist, without a shadow of a doubt. But if you were to ask her, she probably wouldn't know what on earth you're talking about. She would just tell you about her passion for the job and how it empowered her to perform at a consistently high level. Her love of teaching shone through in everything she did for both her students and her colleagues. The result was that parents contacted the school's principal months before the start of the new school year in an attempt to reserve a place for their child in my mother's class.

Yes, she may have been stressed at times about certain events (first communion, school trips, parents' evening, etc.), but it was never harmful stress. It was pure excitement and a burning desire to get things right, to make it the best possible experience for everyone. Yes, that *is* perfectionism, but it's the good kind. She didn't need to prove anything to herself or anyone. Working diligently was natural to her. She wasn't a slave to the system but reveled in the freedom she had created for herself by living her passion.

In my coaching work, I see so many people who are working their socks off to impress others or themselves for that matter. Sometimes they are working incredibly hard to cover up emotional issues that need to be addressed. That's when perfectionism becomes a neurotic reaction and throws you off balance. That's when you can fall ill and become depressed. You will really benefit from letting go of desperately trying to achieve perfection. You know it doesn't serve you, and you hate the feeling, so why continue like this?

At the outset of a new project—whether it's writing your memoirs, finding the perfect house, or planning your wedding—simply embark upon the task with the intention of doing the best possible job. That's all. Be clear about your intentions, then flow forward by enjoying each easy or difficult step along the way.

All you need to focus on is doing a good job. Detach yourself from the outcome. Your detachment doesn't mean you don't care. It means you trust yourself and the process. You can obviously influence your own thoughts, but you can't be responsible for someone else's opinion about your work. Everybody is entitled to form their own opinions. Many people might like your work and some people might not, but it's their free choice to miss out on what you are offering. When you can internalize that knowledge, that's when you are detached from the outcome.

This book you're holding in your hands right this minute is an example of positive perfectionism. At the outset, the prospect of writing a new book is both exciting and overwhelming. It's exciting because it's such a powerful way of sharing my ideas with you, but it's overwhelming because it's such a large project. This is where my attitude—my mental approach—will make the difference between negative stress and positive perfectionism throughout the writing process.

At the start of every chapter, before I write down a single word, I take a moment to get into my spiritual coaching zone. I frame my perfectionism by letting go of needing to write the right material. This would only create negative energy, blocking me rather than inspiring me. I get clear on what I want to tell my readers. I ask myself (and the Universe during meditation) what people might like to know, what they would like to receive guidance on. By turning negative stress into positive perfectionism, I increase my creative energy. Inspiration flows effortlessly and turns the book project into a very enjoyable experience for me. When I feel stuck, I recognize what's happening and quickly take a step back. By giving myself space to breathe and refocus, I stay in the flow and make sure I get the most joy from writing. And I do!

In addition, I can maintain my inner peace by realizing that some people will resonate with some parts of my work and other people will resonate with other parts. Rather than allow this particular fact of writing life to slow me down, I accept it. I believe in being authentic in what I say or do and allowing others to draw their own conclusions. Different social, cultural, and religious influences often play a major role in this and create, in turn, wonderful learning opportunities for readers to think outside their own particular boxes and release dogmatic beliefs that no longer serve them. When my favorite singer releases a new album, although

I may not like every single track, I still love the quality of her voice. The artist's intention is to create something beautiful, but different fans will like different songs. It's all a matter of personal taste and preference.

In other words, it's your attitude that will make or break your peace of mind. You can, of course, change your attitude. You can choose to enjoy your work or to let it drag you down. If you need help with changing your attitude, that help is available, and it's up to you to reach out for it.

Family

It's 4:30 in the morning on a Thursday in December. I'm rather cold, but it's not because of the temperature at this time of year. It's because of the air-conditioning in the departures area of Dubai International Airport. I am UK bound after having spent two wonderful days in this dynamic city hosting various coaching seminars. I may be feeling content, but my body clock is all over the place.

I'm still wondering why I was picked up so early from my hotel. My flight doesn't leave until 9:00 a.m., and the drive from my hotel to the airport only took 10 minutes. Only God knows how much time in my life I've spent waiting in airports, but I'm pretty sure it's more than enough to build a small city. For some unknown reason and despite the fact it's so early in the morning, I'm not that bothered having to wait this time.

There's a fascinating energy in the air, and I enjoy the buzz created by all the passengers in the terminal doing their duty-free Christmas shopping. Airports are such wonderful places to observe people from all over the world with their different cultures and faiths. I see an African woman from the Ivory Coast who's delighted to have her picture taken with a cute white toddler who appears to be the son of a young Swiss couple in transit between Australia and Zurich. The scene puts a smile on the tired faces of everyone who passes by. As I'm watching, I can't help but marvel at the wonder of it all. This little child sitting on the arm of an adult is amused by the flashing lights of the cameras and has no idea what life has in store for him.

Or does he?

I'm inspired to turn waiting time into writing time.

You'd be surprised how many clients come to me with family issues and how universal those concerns are. I'm not a qualified family therapist and therefore won't attempt to unravel family dynamics or talk about family psychology. Instead, I'd like to offer a fresh perspective on some family issues through the lens of practical spirituality.

As you have probably guessed by now, there's a reason why your family setup is the way it is. Your family plays an important role in the advancement of your soul during your current incarnation. Now, before I expand on this, feel free to replace the word "family" with friends, work colleagues, or any other group of people with whom you frequently interact. If I talk about a demanding mother, for example, but you recognize one of your friends or work mates, then by all means use my suggestions to create a more positive relationship with that person. All these relationships create perfect canvases for your soul to gain valuable life experience.

As for our families, I really do believe that we choose our parents. We also select our brothers and sisters, and every other member of the clan before we come here to experience life on this planet. You may recall when I talked about growing up in my brother's shadow, I said I believe our souls chose to incarnate together. If this is the first time you are being exposed to this concept, it might sound a little bit odd, but please just keep an open mind.

Think for a moment how impractical it would be for a soul with an agenda for this life to be born into just any random family. What's the use in that? It would be like boarding a train bound for any old destination and not necessarily the one you have chosen for this particular journey. Selecting your family is a very conscious decision made by your soul after careful consideration and in alignment with the learning opportunities that the soul sets for itself for the journey ahead.

Your family is an incredibly effective institute for spiritual learning, and its composition sets the scene for the spiritual growth of all its members. As we've discussed previously, your personal and spiritual growth is a result of undergoing many different experiences during your life. Now, consider the myriad of experiences and learning opportunities that come with your family. What a bonus!

Whether you get along with your family members or they drive you insane, there's always plenty to learn. And the quicker you learn, the sooner you can advance your spiritual growth. In other words, there is value for you in your family dynamics and lots of it! However, if you're currently stuck in a very challenging situation, it will take time, willingness, and patience to appreciate that there's a bigger picture to everything you are experiencing.

For example, if you are subjected to mental or physical abuse, the wounds can be so deep you may not know how to begin to turn the situation around. As always, be gentle and patient with yourself. Gently awaken to the realization that you are a magnificent divine being. Remind yourself often that you are a part of the Universal God Source, that you are a beautiful soul on an immense journey. Be willing to accept and use your God-given power to finally break free from your precarious situation.

You see, even when you resonate with the spiritual idea that you are a soul on a journey and that you have set out to encounter certain events during your lifetime, it doesn't mean you need to stay stuck in any given situation. It's misguided to think, "Oh well, maybe it was the choice of my soul to experience this abuse," and then choose to continue to suffer in silence. Even though you will undoubtedly learn a great deal and evolve as a result of experiencing an abusive situation, an even greater learning opportunity lies in *overcoming* the abuse. That's the twofold nature of spiritual growth.

When you've eventually gathered enough courage to make the decision that it's time to be treated with respect, I promise you the rewards will be sweet. Not only will you be able to start afresh and surround yourself with the respect and love you deserve, but you will also be able to look back and say, "I did well. My soul learned from the abuse, and it's learned even more from breaking free."

Earlier I mentioned that every member of a family will benefit on a soul level from the learning opportunities that present themselves during family dynamics. That's why each of them chose to be born into that specific family. It's not uncommon for souls to continue to incarnate together in pairs or small groups over a number of lifetimes. They will each take on different roles to further their own learning and to give the other souls a chance to complete their schooling mission.

Maria came to me for help with her daughter-in-law Ann. The two women had never been exactly the best of friends, but recently the situation had become almost unbearable. Maria wanted to find a way to dissolve the barriers between Ann and herself quickly.

It became evident that the core of the problem between them was that Maria couldn't resist interfering in Ann's household. Maria was adamant Ann should be more grateful for her help. However, Ann was tired of Maria getting too involved with her life. She did everything in her power to make family get-togethers an unpleasant experience for Maria by pretending Maria wasn't there.

I intuitively picked up that Maria and Ann had experienced other past lives together. In fact, even though they certainly weren't the best of friends in this lifetime, they were actually soul friends who helped each other evolve every time they incarnated together. Maria seemed to resonate strongly with this idea, almost to her own surprise. Her rational mind couldn't quite understand the concept, but it made sense to her on a soul level. Maria had often wondered why Ann disliked her so much, and here was the missing piece of the puzzle. In their current lifetime together, Ann provides Maria an opportunity to resist the temptation to get involved in someone else's affairs and to mind her own business instead.

Incarnating together over many lifetimes doesn't mean our souls take on the same role every time. In other words, your mother could have been your son in a past life or any other relationship you can think of. How many lives two or more souls will embark upon together depends on the evolutionary stage of each of the souls.

As I mentioned before, this dynamic stretches further than just family. Your best friend or worst enemy may well be a soul you know and with whom you have an agreement to incarnate together a number of times. That's why sometimes you meet someone, and there's an instant familiarity. If it feels like you've known them forever, you probably have!

Similarly, you and a soul friend may agree to play very specific roles in order to ensure that either or both of you experience a very specific dynamic. For example, if you don't learn to stand up to your enemy, you may keep on finding yourself in comparable situations in different lifetimes until you do stand up for yourself. And the chances are your enemy will be the same soul reincarnating with you. So do everyone a favor. Honor your soul by refusing to play the victim role any longer and let your soul friend stop having to play the role of enemy!

It's a fascinating concept, isn't it? I realize it may sound extraordinary, especially when we look at some of the horror that goes on in this world. But please give it some thought anyway. The next time you find yourself in a potentially awkward situation with a family member, look at what's going on from this new perspective. You will feel more composed and confident, and that is almost certainly going to attract a better outcome. And if they don't like that you are managing to stay so calm, that's their issue and not yours. You can hold your head high, your dignity intact. Trust me. It's an incredibly good feeling.

Now please don't run to your foes after reading this, shouting, "It's all good! We are all souls on a wondrous journey together!" I'm not sure that's terribly helpful. Simply decide to look at your relationships differently and appreciate the learning potential in those relationships for everyone. Knowing what you now know will help you react less defensively, for example, but you will also have more courage to establish healthy boundaries when required and to break those patterns that no longer serve you.

A Controlling Mother

A while ago I received a question by e-mail from Alina. She wrote the following:

Dear Christoph,
Is there a limit where your mum can control you and your life, or to what age is it still acceptable? I'm 29 years old. Thank you.

Alina, Newcastle upon Tyne, UK.

Dear Alina,
Thank you for your wonderful question. As you are using the word "acceptable," I assume the way your mother exercises control over you is quite firm. There may be multiple reasons why she is so controlling of you. It seems to me that the obvious one would be love. She loves you very much, and to her this is the best way of showing you. There's a good chance

she's copied this style from her own mother. She is not alone in this, since unfortunately many parents "suffocate" their children by using control as a way of demonstrating their love. This often goes on long after the children have reached adulthood.

Another reason could be that she is disappointed with her own life. Sometimes parents want their children to have better options than they had at the same age. This is admirable but, again, the way they go about it might be a bit clumsy. Whatever the reason, at 29 you are certainly at an age where you have every right to want your mother to change her behavior towards you.

And this change can happen, but I'm going to ask *you* to take charge here, Alina. I've had the honour of helping many people your age whose life is being controlled by their parents. They put their stamp on virtually every decision their son or daughter makes. What I'm about to share with you is by no means the only way to resolve the situation with your mum, nor is it a quick fix.

The method I am going to describe is one I've used in the past myself, especially in delicate situations with my parents (e.g., telling them something private about my life). This approach will take a lot of love and patience on your part. But rest assured it's a very good way of paving the way to a more balanced relationship between the two of you, and you will both benefit tremendously.

Alina, I would like to suggest that you consider becoming a *beacon of light* for your mother. In many ways, you need to be a mum for your mum. This may seem like a tall order, but the Universe will provide you with the energy and serenity you require on this journey of emotional healing—healing for both you and your mum. Of course you could go into this situation like most people would do—rebelling and fighting. However, this could make things escalate and potentially damage the relationship with your mum beyond repair.

Our life's journey offers all of us remarkable opportunities for spiritual growth, Alina. They arise from the moment we arrive here on Earth. On a soul level, you and your mum have made a bond to experience life together during this lifetime (and probably many more). As a human being, you grow older and don't remember this agreement you and your mother made before you came here. As a *spiritual human being,* however, you are invited to remember this union of souls and to heal any difficult situation in your life by applying this understanding. Please remember that this is never a responsibility you have to take on. You are empowered to make your own decisions in life, and you are welcome to move forward with this situation in any way you choose.

Cherishing the concept of you and your mum being two beautiful souls, however, will enable you to gently detach from the anxiety caused by her controlling behaviour, and you can take your place in the observer's seat. You'll be able to look at the relationship with your mum with a clear head from the outside, rather than feeling trapped inside it and being upset.

Taking a step back doesn't mean you stop showing your appreciation for your mum. What you are doing is shielding yourself from her controlling energy. By remaining calm, especially loving, and patient, you are holding up a mirror that reflects her heavy energy back without letting it affect you.

Try it for a while, and affirm to yourself often that you are good person and a loving daughter. After some time, you will notice your mum's conduct towards you will begin to change. She will notice her usual controlling style no longer seems to impact you in the way it used to. This will be a confusing experience for her, and I suggest you keep focused on the process of spiritual growth that is taking place. For that's what it is, my friend. Thanks to your willingness, initiative, and wisdom, you are offering your mum the most incredible gift—the opportunity to advance her soul. And in doing so, you are offering your own soul the same gift.

First, by agreeing to be her daughter in this lifetime, you allowed your mum a chance to experience what controlling feels like. Second, by being a spiritual catalyst for change, you present her with the ultimate opportunity to overcome her current behavior—a behavior which is causing her to suffer too, perhaps more than you may realize.

So, Alina, by being a beacon of light, you are setting yourself and your mum free. And what a beautiful way forward it is! As the new balance in energy between the two of you is being established, a new chapter will bloom, and both your souls will be eternally grateful to you for having taken on your challenging spiritual assignment and for completing it so beautifully.

Much light,
Christoph

As we come to the end of this chapter, I realize that there are many more things people worry about on a daily basis. Today's world can indeed be very demanding, and we face many adversities. Many of these will have external triggers (e.g., money), but often the greatest challenges we face lie within ourselves. In this chapter, I have endeavored to show you a different way to approach these concerns.

You really are a divine being. That doesn't mean you should start behaving as if you were God's gift to humanity. Just be open to the idea that you are, indeed, God's gift to yourself. Simply stretching your mind a little bit further will be enough to begin your transformation. Everyday happiness and zestful living can become a reality for you by changing the way you look at your life and yourself. Respect yourself and let go of those stressful and self-deprecating thoughts, emotions, and behaviors. If you're willing to put in that effort, step into your role as a divine creator, and accept your personal power, the Universe will meet you halfway and cocreate with you.

Summary of This Chapter

- Loving yourself is not selfish; *not* loving yourself is.
- Heal your anger by changing your attitude toward whatever makes you angry. It's your attitude that will make or break your peace of mind. Small changes in your attitude will make huge changes in your life.
- Letting go of guilt is a fast track to happiness. Whatever you may be worrying about, if it wasn't your deliberate intention to hurt someone or to cause a certain outcome, then just let it go.
- Any jealousy you have of other people's success will only slow down your own.
- You are in a soul relationship with all the significant people in your life. You help their soul to advance, and they help yours. Remember this when times are hard.
- The day you realize you are a magnificently beautiful being will be the day you'll stop needing others to tell you so. And you will be free.
- It's not about climbing up the stairway of life. It's about climbing down the steps into your heart.

The funny thing about this luxury called inner happiness is that it's totally free and available in abundance.
If we learn how to make it through each day in a meaningful way, daily happiness will flow as a result.

CHAPTER 5

Powerful Happiness Habits

Imagine you wake up in the morning. The sun is shining in your bedroom window. The birds are chirping. You just love this time of day. All is calm, peaceful, and serene—and so are you. You feel great, and you have only just opened your eyes. You feel positive, and you're happy to wake up to another promising day full of opportunities, joy, and excitement.

A gentle sense of grace envelops you, as it does every morning. It always feels so magical. You feel one with the Universe. You love this feeling of being protected, safe, and not alone. Feeling rejuvenated, you are pleased to discover that you now have the answer to that thorny problem at work that's been on your mind. It feels as if you have received guidance, support, and answers during your sleep. What a great way to start the day with this kind of clarity!

Throughout your day you feel in control, and you are able to let go of any stressful thoughts. You can think empowering thoughts easily. There is plenty of room for fun and laughter in your day. You appear radiant, confident, and self-assured because you know how to stay on your chosen path. You feel inspired and love working on your dreams and goals. You intuitively know which steps are best for you to take, as if you carry the map of your life in your hands. The emotional freedom is incredible. It makes you feel really great about yourself. You have lots of energy, and you receive compliments on your vitality. Your positive outlook on life and your optimism are inspirational and attract many wonderful people and opportunities to you.

Is this too good to be true? Do you believe you could never in a million years create that kind of day for yourself? Are you having a hard time wrapping your arms around the idea that this could be the way you live your life? I totally understand. But here's the good news. All this and more is possible. Creating this kind of life and this kind of happiness on a daily basis is within your grasp, and I'm going to show you how to do it. I do it every day for myself, and so can you. And here's why I can say this so confidently.

I discovered a long time ago that happiness is an inside job, not an outside job. Happiness doesn't depend on money, love, fame, weather, health, etc.—externals that can sometimes be out of our control. It's all about the internals and taking action. Happiness doesn't have to be this way-out-there thing you never achieve. It becomes a choice you can make for yourself.

Someone once asked me, "You seem to be happy all the time, even when things don't go well. What's your secret?" I replied by saying I am a contented person who understands why adversities show up in my life, that I want to overcome them to aid my spiritual growth, and that I have found some really great ways to do so. My contentment generates a genuine happiness, self-respect, and enthusiasm for my life. I believe that's what people notice about me, perhaps because it is relatively rare unfortunately. But it doesn't have to be rare in your life.

Making the most of an ordinary day is how you create a happy life. After all, you experience far more ordinary than extraordinary days in your life. And there are ways to transform the ordinary into the extraordinary every single day. You can learn how to do this.

This is how I get the most out of a typical day. Imagine a beautiful roof. Make it sturdy, shining, and give it a beautiful design. Got it? The roof symbolizes your happiness, and it is constructed on top of solid walls. In fact, the walls need to be in place first, right? These walls are what it is all about. They're special. They support your roof of genuine happiness and inner peace.

In my own life, the four walls supporting my inner peace are connection, affection, direction, and action. To keep my roof of happiness in place, I want to consistently check to be sure my supporting walls are in place. These walls are, in fact, habits. Powerful habits that I honor daily; positive habits that have made my life so much better. These habits make me feel protected, healthy, empowered, and in control of my life.

Habit 1: Connection

Reaffirming My Relationship with the Universe and My Guides

When you are asleep, your soul occasionally embarks on an astral trip to visit different realms beyond our physical world. Just as your body rejuvenates during sleep, your soul revitalizes when it detaches from your physical body. One of the places to which your soul returns for a brief time is the astral world. This usually happens when it feels the need to "cuddle with God," so to speak. Perhaps your soul feels stuck and yearns for guidance or clarification on the challenges it is facing. Or perhaps your soul simply wants to receive validation that it's doing a great job during its current incarnation on Earth.

No matter how incredibly strong, amazing, and all-knowing your soul might be, it too benefits from reassurance and rejuvenation by spending quality time in the presence of the God Source. If you wake up in the morning with a bright idea or more clarity about a concern you've had, then there's a good chance your soul has been on a little trip to the astral world to get some coaching.

When your soul is away from the body while you're asleep, you are always protected by higher forces. So please don't worry your soul might not make it back into your body. Having said that, when I wake up, I'm always grateful to realize I am alive and breathing and to know the soul part of me is safely connected back with the body part of me, regardless of whether my soul has journeyed the night before or not.

Not only is waking up a moment for which to be grateful, it's also a powerful moment. Any concerns I may have had on my mind before I fell asleep seem to be a lot lighter or they have cleared altogether. And the rest of my day still lies ahead of me. It's a magical moment, and it always fills me with excitement. Every morning I think to myself, "There are so many things I will know by the time I go to bed tonight that I don't know yet. I simply cannot wait to find out what will happen in my world today!"

This is my golden opportunity to set myself up for having a great day. I believe in easing my mind into the day ahead and setting the tone of that day with a gentle, free-flow meditation. This is why waking up is such a powerful part of the day. I gear myself up for a day filled with learning, joy, and contentment. "Uh oh. Meditation? In the morning? I don't have time for that."

I hear you. Yes, I do meditate in the morning. But did you hear me say it has to last for half an hour? No. My morning meditation is short. It is easy, practical, and uplifting. It only takes me a few moments to thank the Universe and my spirit guides for keeping me safe during my sleep. I also thank them in advance for protecting and guiding me throughout my upcoming day.

I tell the Universe and my guides that I am looking forward to fully using the potential of the day ahead and that I am willing to grow emotionally, mentally, and spiritually. In addition, I ask for energy, strength, and assistance so I can be the best possible support and guide for the people I work with that day. All this gives me a wonderful feeling of being connected to the bigger picture. When I think about how I'm a part of the Universal God Source and that I have a team of spiritual guides looking out for me, I feel privileged to be in such excellent company.

Let's talk about spirit guides for a moment. All of us have one or more spirit guides and, as you can probably guess, that relationship is a prearranged agreement between souls. Only in this case your spirit guides, unlike the souls who journey to Earth with you, remain in the astral world. Before you are born, you and your spirit guides decide to complete this spiritual assignment called life together. You are all in full agreement and understanding of the path you will walk during your lifetime here.

People often refer to spirit guides as guardian angels, but that's misleading. They aren't angels. Spirit guides are spiritual beings who have accumulated experience by incarnating on this Earth one or more lifetimes. In other words, spirit guides really understand what you are going through because they've been here. They've walked in your shoes, so to speak.

When you have a moment to yourself, talk to your guides out loud. You don't need to be a psychic or a medium to communicate with them. You may not hear them audibly, but they can certainly hear you. Spirit guides will always respect your free will and therefore don't usually interfere with your life unless they're asked to do so. When you do call on their guidance and help, be specific.

Be open to receiving answers in many different ways. Perhaps your answer will be displayed on a billboard, or it will be something you hear on radio or television. It may be contained in a book or magazine you are reading. Perhaps a friend will say something, or maybe you'll just receive spontaneous inspiration and wonder why you didn't think of that before. You will know in your heart when you've received the answer to the question you've asked, and I encourage you to trust your heart's guidance on this.

Find a quiet moment to talk to your spirit guides out loud about your fears and dreams. Let them know you are willing to do your part, and then put in some effort to do exactly that. This isn't about just asking and sitting back, waiting to receive. This is about you doing the footwork, knowing you will receive assistance. When you cocreate your life with your spiritual helpers, you don't need to feel alone ever again.

A while ago, it was recommended I have some simple surgery done on my nose. The nose bone was growing slightly sideways, often obstructing the flow of air in my right nostril, and it had become rather annoying, especially since my work involves public speaking. Now, as much as I could see the benefit of having the operation, I was absolutely terrified of the general anesthetic required. I knew I didn't have much of a choice, but I can honestly say I was anxious beyond belief.

As someone who likes very much to be in control of his life and who isn't the best or soundest of sleepers, I struggled with the idea that they were going to "switch me off" during the surgical procedure. They would have power over me, and I didn't like that one bit. Also, I was dreading waking up feeling the worse for wear. Suffice it to say I was creating quite the fire-breathing dragon in my head.

I was given a date for the operation, and all I could do was prepare myself as best as I could. I read up on how a general anesthetic was administered and what patients had to say about it. But there was only so much the Internet could do for me, and I knew it was time to turn to those who would understand my irrational fear—my spirit guides.

One afternoon, I retreated to my bedroom, and I asked out loud for my guides to please remove this anxiety and for them to stay close to me during my operation. Later that evening I was at the gym, when suddenly the most beautiful song started playing on the radio. I recalled hearing it before. The song was *Run* by Leona Lewis, and I was deeply moved by the chorus lyrics. *"Even if you cannot hear my voice, I'll be right beside you, Dear."*

I fell in love with the song immediately, downloaded it, and listened to it over and over again, almost obsessively. And then, all of a sudden, I realized what was actually happening. My spirit guides were, in fact, answering the desperate cry for help I had made a few hours earlier! *"Even if you cannot hear my voice, I'll be right beside you, Dear."*

I was both astonished and overcome with joy at the same time. You see, spirit guides will use seemingly trivial yet rather amazing ways of reaching out to you. All you need to do is be open-minded and willing to see it. So, when the anesthetist gently prepared my arm to put me under, I fell asleep to the very comforting knowledge (and melody) that my guides were right beside me.

I can't recommend too highly building a relationship with the Universe and your guides. It might just be the boost and support you've been longing for, and it will give you that feeling of not being on your own in this game called life. Your life will become so much more enjoyable when you endeavor to include your spiritual helpers in it.

Don't just build this relationship during your meditations, but maintain and foster this connection as much as possible throughout your day. A real and honest spiritual relationship with your guides and the Universe will truly lift you during challenging times and make the good times that much more extraordinary. As you evolve and recognize the help you have enjoyed from higher realms, there will be an added dimension to your success and happiness. And the more you express your gratitude, the more you will feel this support, guidance, and grace on your path.

Your meditations with the Universe and your team of spiritual helpers don't just have to take place when you wake up. Since they only take a few moments, you can do them regularly. Sometimes you'll be connecting and expressing your gratitude. Other times you'll be seeking answers or asking for clarification. The point is you will be making connection throughout your day. My own favorite times to get in touch are when I'm driving, taking a shower, walking in nature, feeling particularly grateful or touched by grace, and just before falling asleep at night.

Habit 2: Affection

Being Kind to My Mind

I make a deliberate decision to demonstrate my affection for my mind by being as kind to my mind as possible. This resolution plays a huge role in the "secret" to my happiness. Being kind to my mind is a way of self-appreciation I have finally mastered after many years of being harsh with myself and hammering away at my mind with self-destructive thoughts. As you read further, you will learn how you too can be more kind to your mind, and I promise you will be amazed at and love the difference it makes to your inner happiness!

Being kind to your mind is about making a choice. A choice to think kinder thoughts that will positively serve you rather than upset or paralyze you with fear, doubt, or anxiety. You can gently and effectively train your mind to create kind thoughts that will make you happier and boost your self-esteem. After a little time spent training yourself, you will notice that thinking kind thoughts becomes a powerful and positive habit.

This is not just about thinking happy thoughts, nor am I suggesting that you should ever try to fool yourself by thinking thoughts with which you don't resonate. Also, if you suffer from depressing thoughts most of the time, you might find it helpful to consult your doctor or another qualified professional. What I'm talking about here is placing more *constructive* thoughts in your mind. Constructive thoughts can help you alleviate your self-doubt and fearful thinking as well as clear your inner state. And it's more easily achieved than you might think. You are designing a joyous mindset for yourself by actively thinking thoughts that are uplifting, positive, and creative. You will start to feel balanced, evened out, and in control.

I do it all the time. Throughout my day I will use positive, loving thoughts to help me banish any stress I might feel. For example, let's say I've just received a phone call asking if I would be interested in doing a talk on spiritual living to a huge group of people. My initial response is, "Fantastic!" My second reaction is I need to find the nearest chair and sit down. I'm thinking, "Oh my goodness, am I crazy? Why do I always do this to myself? I'm petrified!"

But then I choose to think more heartening thoughts. "This is what I love to do, and I did well last time. This is another beautiful opportunity to share my joy with the world. There's a reason why they chose me, and I honor the compliment by choosing to enjoy the experience." Within a short period of time, I feel peaceful again.

Here's another example. I pick up my car after an engine service, and the bill is three times higher than I expected. I can dwell on that and let it drag me down, or I can choose to think more uplifting thoughts. "At least my car will be safe again, and I deserve to be safe. My car will be worth even more if I decide to sell it."

Do you see what I'm doing here? I'm not running away from things. I am simply choosing to refocus any unpleasant or disturbing thoughts toward the positive instead, thereby creating more peace of mind for myself.

It takes courage to take a closer look at your thinking. Many people run away from this challenge as if their lives depended on it! They look for constant distraction in order to not be forced to address their thinking patterns. They'll grasp at magazines, movies, shopping, cleaning—anything to keep them occupied and protected from whatever they don't really want to think about. That's a pretty powerful indication that addressing thinking patterns is difficult.

Here's a question for you. If all the thoughts you have on an average day were printed in a book, would you want to read that book? Or would you rather burn it? Take a moment to look at your thinking pattern. Are you kind to your mind? Or are most of your thoughts fearful? Self-critical? Is your glass always half empty or half full? If you're tired of listening to your inner, energy-zapping voices of despair and negative chatter, get into a habit of thinking constructive thoughts. Think up positive solutions to your problems, even if those solutions are future based.

Maybe you long to travel the world, for example, but you don't have the budget to do so at the moment. You could feel sad about that and say to yourself, "It will never happen for me." And there is indeed a good chance that's true if you continue thinking that way. A better option is to decide to steer away from pessimism and affirm instead, "I welcome being able to travel the world someday soon." You may even want to follow up this powerful statement by asking the Universe and your guides to assist you with this. Remember, if you don't *ask* they won't know! That's how you can shift from being your own worst enemy to being your mind's best friend.

Another very effective way to be kind to your mind is to bring a little bit of humor into your life. I do this as often as I can. Being interested in spirituality doesn't mean I don't allow myself to be silly and enjoy a good laugh. If you have been under too much stress lately or you've overloaded your mind with negative thinking, you can restore balance by adding a little humor. It can really lift you back up.

Humor is a wonderful remedy for stress because it releases endorphins in your brain. Laughter is indeed the best medicine. A good laugh with your friends can work miracles. I mean the kind of laugh where tears are pouring down your cheeks, you're gasping for breath, and your stomach hurts. Seriously, when was the last time you laughed yourself silly about something?

Another suggestion I would like to make is to be open to receiving a compliment once in a while. You deserve to be acknowledged for your skills and talents. So the next time someone gives you a compliment, don't try to fend it off because you think you're not worthy of receiving recognition. You are valued and really do deserve compliments. Allow others to praise you. Similarly, I encourage you to give compliments to others more often. Knowing that criticism immediately knocks people off balance and that compliments tend to lift them up, how many people will you compliment tomorrow?

Habit 3: Direction

I Monitor If I'm on Track

A while ago, my friend Simon asked if I would go shopping with him. He hates spending time in the shopping mall on his own but urgently needed a new suit for a job interview. So off we went, our sights set on finding the perfect suit and excited because we hadn't seen each other for a while. My fashion-conscious friend knew precisely what he wanted—a gray striped suit with a modern cut.

We visited some of the finest designer shops in the mall, and Simon looked at different suits. In the meantime, we were talking all the time, solving the world's problems. Simon managed to accumulate quite a pile of jackets and trousers to be tried on. However, we became so engrossed in our conversation about his exciting new career plans that we decided we needed a place to sit down and have a proper chat. So we forgot all about the clothes and went to the nearby Starbucks instead. After all, we could always go back to get his suit after we'd had our chat and our coffee, right? You've probably already guessed what happened or didn't happen. We had a terrific afternoon catching up, but we left without Simon's suit.

This pattern often repeats itself in life. It's easy to get offtrack. It's easy to become distracted and forget what we set out to do or what we wanted to accomplish, however large or small. So that's why I check every day to be sure I'm on track. This habit is about asking myself the right questions.

As a life coach, I'm well aware of the impact effective questioning can have. A powerful question has the potential to solicit an equally powerful and incredibly useful answer. The right question can inspire insight, inner wisdom, and creative solutions neither my coaching client nor I have thought of before. That's why I ask myself powerful questions often. I know the answers are my compass, enabling me to take corrective action if I've gotten offtrack.

Here are some powerful coaching questions you can use to help you reflect on your aspirations, challenges, and obstacles. You can also use them as a template to come up with your own questions. Make sure your questions are open-ended (can't be answered by a simple yes or no) so you are forced to think on a deeper level. This activates your creativity and your ability to draw upon all of your resources.

> *What do I want to achieve and how am I doing?*
> *What's happened so far?*
> *What's working well?*
> *What's not working so well? Why not?*
> *What can I eliminate/decrease? Where? How?*
> *What can I include/increase? Where? How?*
> *Where can I find help?*
> *How can I be there for myself?*
> *What's the next step?*
> *What does success look like?*

We are usually very good at pointing out what's going wrong, what's not working, and where the lack is. However, the way out of this limited, problem-oriented thinking is to ask ourselves powerful, open-ended questions that stimulate us to think in options and solutions instead. I use these powerful questions every day to monitor my own personal progress in all areas of my life—personal, professional, leisure, finances, physical surroundings, spiritual growth.

In that way, I become my own coach and hold myself accountable for my actions and the results of those actions. It helps me identify where I might need to make some changes. And if I'm not happy about something in my life, I don't feel the need to blame anyone for it because I realize I can do something about it. In fact, I'm the only one who *can* do anything about it.

Asking myself the right self-coaching questions contributes to my daily happiness because it empowers me to live with increased awareness. It helps me stay in top form emotionally, spiritually, and physically so I can create the top form life I deserve. I encourage you to do the same.

Take a few moments now to reflect on your track and your progress along that track. Your track can be a specific short- or long-term project or perhaps a treasured dream. See where you are doing really well, but also identify those areas where you are not achieving the results you intended. Now ask yourself some good open-ended questions to get you going again and help you feel inspired from within. This powerful technique is about revisiting your original plans and making small adjustments where required. Do this without judging and criticizing yourself. Love and respect yourself instead.

Habit 4: Action

Taking Care of My Body

I am not a vain person, but I can take my shirt off at the beach and feel good about it. (In fact, I'm at the beach now on holiday, so I am particularly motivated to write about this topic.) I used to be skinny and didn't have much spare energy because I was a heavy smoker. I've invested a lot of time and energy in changing that situation and feeling this confident about my body.

It takes consistent effort and time to shape up. Whoever says you can make it happen in a matter of weeks has never set foot in a gym, believe me. This book is about getting your life in shape. But if you have always wanted to get your body in shape too, then this section is for you. That doesn't mean I'm going to write a treatise on the benefits of physical activity or give you a selection of tailor-made exercise programs. There are plenty of other books that do that. I only want this book to give you strength. And that could include the strength to make positive changes to your body as well as to your life.

I want to motivate you to motivate yourself to take action—to include some kind of physical activity in your life. Whether it's enjoying an hour at the gym, attending yoga sessions, taking walks in nature, or attending a dance class, explore the option that's right for you and start releasing those endorphins! Endorphins are the body's natural chemicals that are released during physical activity. They are excellent stress, fatigue, and pain relievers.

For me, the gym is a place of inspiration. I can sit in front of my computer all day working on an article and trying to find the right words, but sometimes nothing flows. Then I decide to go for a good gym session and, before I know it, I need to ask someone for pen and paper because I get idea after idea, and I want to write everything down before I forget it. I'm fortunate because my gym overlooks a beautiful waterfront area. So it's a particularly terrific place for me to connect with the Universe and my guides and to reflect and receive inspiration.

If you think you don't have the time to work out or get involved in some other kind of physical activity, I urge you to think again. Many people have very crowded schedules, but they still manage to exercise on a regular basis. How do they do it? They want it badly enough so they make time for it. Being healthier and looking and feeling better are so important to them they make physical activity a priority. They understand and want to continue to experience the incredible physical and emotional benefits of keeping fit. So no matter how busy their lives might be, they will create time for exercise. It really is that simple.

My brother is an excellent example of someone who prioritizes exercise in his life. Philip is a senior executive at a major international company, and his schedule is hectic at best. He's one of those businessmen who flies halfway across the planet to attend a half-hour meeting to sign a multimillion dollar contract. On Monday, Philip might be in San Francisco and on Tuesday in Frankfurt. On Wednesday, I receive a text message telling me he's about to board a flight to Paris for a last-minute convention.

Yet, despite the heavy demands of his work, Philip finds the time for regular workouts. Why? Because he understands the value of keeping fit. He is well aware that without maintaining his energy levels, he would find it difficult to continue being so productive. How does he do it? He has found a unique way of making physical exercise something to look forward to and of combining two priorities in one activity.

Philip has three young children, and spending time with them is of prime importance to him. However, he doesn't sit with them in front of the television. He plays tennis and football with them, takes them for walks, and goes with them to their swimming classes. My brother really understands the importance of spending time with his children as well as the importance of physical activity. I admire how he manages to honor these two priorities in his busy life by combining them and how he is passing on his values and priorities to his children.

If you don't think you can be torn away from your favorite television show or your precious reading time on the sofa, let me assure you that you can watch television while shaping up on the treadmill (or any other equipment for that matter). I too love reading, and it's something I often do when I'm at the gym or out walking or running. I listen to audio books, inspirational podcasts, and so forth. This way I can optimize my time by learning and getting inspired while engaging in physical exercise.

In this chapter, I have shared with you the secret to my contentment. You recall the roof analogy I mentioned at the beginning of this chapter. If you want to build a roof, you need to make sure the walls are in place first. The walls that keep my roof of happiness in place are my *connection* to the Universe and my spirit guides, my *affection* for my mind, making sure I continue to flow in the *direction* of my happiness, and taking the *action* of keeping physically active. Those are the four secrets to my contentment.

I can't reiterate enough that *if I can, you can*. Remember that very few things happen overnight in life. I've had to learn these skills, approaches, and self-coaching techniques. It hasn't always been an easy road, but I was very patient with myself all along the way. And I slowly grew more confident. Now that my four powerful habit walls are firmly in place and supporting my roof of happiness, I feel in control and blessed with inner peace. I can look back on my journey so far and say, "It has been more than worth it!"

Summary of This Chapter

- Making the most of every ordinary day is how you create a happy life. Too many simple opportunities for happiness are lost in the process of constant worrying about making more money, climbing the career ladder, meeting the person of your dreams, and so many other things which may or may not happen after all anyway. You've got today, and you're entitled to feeling happy. So use and enjoy this day to the full. Make it an extraordinary day.

- Connect with your spirit guides and reaffirm your connection to the Universal God Source daily. Spiritual help is available, but you need to call on it and have an open mind because the answers and guidance will find you in different ways.

- Be kind to your mind. You can design a joyous mindset for yourself by actively thinking thoughts that are uplifting, enthusiastic, and creative. And then you will feel (and be) balanced and in control.

- Infuse more humor into your life and give more compliments.

- Stay focused and on track. Coach yourself by asking open-ended questions that make you look inside. Use these powerful questions every day to monitor your progress in all areas of your life.

- Make a conscious decision to include physical exercise in your lifestyle. Join a gym, enroll in a yoga class, go for walks in nature. Physical activity releases endorphins in your brain that alleviate stress, pain, fatigue, and anxiety.

Happiness is an inside job; not an outside job. It becomes a choice you can make for yourself.

CHAPTER 6

The Opportunity of
Your Lifetime

Success Guaranteed

Your beautiful and courageous soul takes on human form in order to experience beingness on Planet Earth to aid in its evolution. To incarnate and then live your life is enough to succeed from a spiritual point of view. Success is quite simply defined as being a human being experiencing life here on this planet. No matter what stage of life you are in or how unreal it may seem to you right now, your life *is* a success. To take on a lifetime as a human being in order to advance to a higher level of consciousness is a big deal for your soul. The miracle of your incarnation deserves to be considered with pride, respect, and dignity.

I'm surprised when I hear people say, "I'm only human." As if being human is inferior, weak, or pitiful. Too often that statement is used as a justification for an action that didn't turn out as originally planned or an outcome that was unsatisfactory. I believe those who use this expression have little idea how disempowering such a statement really is.

It basically denies their magnificence and instantly reduces their inner power to zero.

Do you sometimes proclaim to the world that you are only human? A more empowering and self-respecting way of looking at "failure" would be recognizing that, no matter what the particular outcome, there is no "only" when it comes to being human. Being human is an extraordinary achievement, including everything you undertake and every outcome that results. I can't emphasize this spiritual reality too much.

Your journey here on Earth is a significant accomplishment. This insight can truly make you reappreciate and revalue your life and therefore shed a brighter light on it. Your presence on this planet is the current physical manifestation of your soul, and so you are a success from the moment you are born.

Moreover, I believe success cannot be measured by looking at someone's great achievements alone. It's too simplistic a measure, yet that is exactly what society does. It seems we have to achieve great things in order to be successful. But what exactly are those great things anyway? Raising a family? Building a fantastic body? Making it on television? What translates as great to me doesn't necessarily translate as great to you. I might think graduating from university is an amazing thing to achieve and therefore makes you a success, but you might think it isn't such a big deal because it was relatively easy for you to accomplish.

Defining success is like defining art—it is a highly subjective experience. Unfortunately the benchmarks of success seem to have been set by society instead of individuals. Even though you don't always resonate with those benchmarks, you still go out of your way to achieve them. You go to great lengths (both consciously and unconsciously) to conform to the norms and expectations set by society, your place of employment, your family, and others, but often to no avail and often at great cost to your emotional and physical health.

In an increasingly demanding world, you are expected to find your vocation, climb the career ladder, look fantastic, live abundantly, marry the perfect spouse, raise model children, etc., etc., etc. Not surprisingly, the pressure that comes with these standards has become unbearable for many people and is a significant cause of stress and anxiety nowadays.

I subscribe to a different way of defining success. It's a liberating perspective I learned on my own journey of self-awakening and spiritual development. Much to my delight, I discovered how success is measured on a spiritual level, making it a thousand times more appealing to me than earthly success.

This invigorating perspective takes the stress out of earthly success for me and is precisely why it has been much easier for me to obtain earthly success and enjoy that success on a whole new level. Success has become appealing again to me, but this time for the right reason—a deep spiritual reason with which I can resonate. This reason gives me something I can believe in, and that's why I passionately share its liberating power with my clients and now with you.

The spiritual perspective on success that I love so much tells us that success is an intimate *review* between you and your soul. It is a sacred engagement. Your soul intrinsically understands your actions and looks at what you accomplish in your life within the framework of your external means, personal capacities, and innate skills and talents. The measure of the success of your life is very different for your soul than for us humans.

This spiritual insight is important to acknowledge because you might be thinking your life doesn't stand for much, and yet your soul is basking in the glory of the totality of your actions large and small. I'm not saying this to make you feel better or to encourage complacency. I'm saying it because this soul perspective was a tonic for me.

I learned to understand and appreciate that all of my actions are precious in the grand scheme of my lifetime. My ups, my downs, my finest hours, my moments of shame, my love, my anger, my support, my reluctance, my challenges—they are all pieces of my life's puzzle. Every piece is a part of my human experience, and I need all of those pieces if I want to put my puzzle together. If you look at the totality of your life this way, then this soul perspective will be a tonic for you too. Your soul is nonjudgmental. It is simply grateful for every experience you go through, for everything you do and create, and for every breath you take. Your soul celebrates the totality of your life for the tremendous success it is. It marvels at the ongoing expansion of your life and your consciousness. Your soul is grateful that you are collecting all your pieces and putting your puzzle together.

Every time I share this soul perspective with lecture audiences or private coaching clients, I ask them to take a moment to look at their lives from this angle. It's one of my favorite exercises because it is a great tool for self-reflection and a real eye-opener. The outcome of this exercise is refreshing for people. There is always a noticeable look of relief on people's faces when they awaken to the realization that there is, in fact, a lot in their lives that could be considered successful. They just needed a fresh perspective on it.

People are soon in awe of the scope of everything they accomplish and how every deed, gesture, experience and outcome—positive or negative—has value and always contributes to their personal and spiritual growth. A seminar guest named Joseph once declared jokingly, "If I look at my life that way, then I'm nothing short of a superhero!" I told him that was precisely the way his soul saw him.

Superhero You

Take a moment now and reflect on the totality of everything you accomplish during an ordinary day. It will surprise you just how successful you are. Think of all those small but wonderful things you do that make *you* a superhero. Safely dropping off the kids at school, walking your dog, helping out a colleague at the office, looking after your elderly parents, caring for your sick friend, engaging in physical exercise, paying your bills on time, etc. *Everything* is a success. Do this exercise often, and be in awe of the success story that is your life.

We are all superheroes. Not all of us can make the headlines or be in the limelight, but that doesn't mean we can't be or aren't successful. A homemaker might not be the CEO of a multinational corporation, but she is tremendously successful at looking after her family and making sure the household runs like clockwork. That is success on a different scale. She is a CEO in her own unique way.

The hard work of a volunteer might go unnoticed, yet a charity organization depends on it. That makes the volunteer's contribution a success. When I worked for Japan Airlines, I noticed that a street sweeper is well respected in Japan, even in a country where the title on a business card means everything. The Japanese believe the street sweeper's work is a success too, for without his help there would be dirty streets. I have always loved that refreshing approach, and I believe we can all learn from it.

Superheroes are everywhere, but they don't always know they're superheroes. Recently a woman named Caroline told me she thought her life wasn't very meaningful. I said that was a rather bold statement and asked her to tell me why she was so convinced of this. Caroline said all she does is work all day in a small bakery shop in the local village—day in, day out. But every morning and evening, before and after her shift and without fail, she stops by the flat of her 84-year-old mother-in-law to make sure she is doing okay. This takes up a lot of Caroline's spare time, but she makes the visits anyway—not only because she wants to, but also because all the other family members live further away.

I told Caroline she was nothing less than a miracle worker for her mother-in-law. She was a light in an elderly person's seemingly endless darkness. I told her she was single-handedly making every day better simply by dropping by and saying hello. Caroline needed to be reminded that her company and care were invaluable, making this elderly woman's days less lonely and that much more special. I assured Caroline her life does have meaning and is a resounding success. I recall the beaming smile this brought to her face when Caroline realized I was right, that her life was indeed meaningful.

When I say, "To be is to succeed," I want to help you set yourself free—free from the suffocating pressure that arises when you think you must make it big in life or attain the nearly impossible to be considered a success. I have said this pressure comes mostly from society, your family, your workplace, or all three. But there's an additional source from where this pressure originates. If you take an honest look inside yourself, you will realize that you are often the source of your greatest stress.

Don't get me wrong—I believe in self-discipline and taking consistent action. I work hard, and I know you do too. The internal stress I want to address here is not the energy that empowers you but the one that disempowers you. It's the negative pressure that holds you back rather than propels you forward, and it is self-inflicted.

Slave Driver

More and more often, I meet people who have become their own slave drivers. They have set extremely high goals and are unreasonably hard on themselves. These people always want more, they want it faster, they expect everyone to keep up with them, they push themselves, they often run before they can walk, they get even more stressed when something doesn't work out, and they are incapable of enjoying their current blessings. Do you recognize yourself in this? Have you been pushing yourself too hard lately, to the point nothing really makes sense anymore? Is a slave driver living inside you?

Let me assure you there is no spiritual value in being unreasonably hard on oneself. It is a waste of your valuable time. Self-analysis is a good thing, but beating yourself up is pointless. Remember you are good enough just the way you are and your life is a success just the way it is. Constantly expecting too much from yourself or disliking yourself when you think you may have failed is unnecessary.

Superheroes know self-punishment doesn't serve them. If they don't achieve the result they want, they respect themselves enough to focus on what they can do differently next time. Nor do they wear themselves out. They are respectful of their energy and use it wisely. Superheroes understand how their life puzzles work. They understand that every outcome they achieve, good and bad, is part of their human experience.

Now is a good time to send your slave driver packing. Make a conscious decision to be kind to yourself by releasing the need to be overly self-critical and goal obsessed. Break out of the cycles that trigger your internal stress and anxiety. You no longer need them. There comes a time when enough is enough. That time is now. Fully open yourself up to the pivotal spiritual reality that your life is already successful. Let go of the pressure to succeed.

Now that your slave driver has been vanquished for good, I want to tell you about the fun twist that comes with awakening to the spiritual meaning of success. It's something I find fascinating, and it gives me that warm cozy feeling inside. It fascinates me because it seems almost contradictory.

I so clearly remember when I learned about the true definition of success. It was a time of significant personal and spiritual growth, and I felt more freedom than I had ever felt before. As I learned that I didn't have to be flawless or achieve perfection to consider my life successful, I began to experience new levels of motivation and energy. It was a deeply transformational phase for me.

I had lived under far too much pressure to succeed for far too long—trying to finish university, find a decent job, be like my brother, etc. When I got some spiritual clarity around success, I realized I didn't *have to* do anything extraordinary. But suddenly that's exactly what I *wanted* to do!

What a positive and exhilarating paradox that was! It was refreshing and stimulating. Everything I did from then on, I did because I wanted to—not because I felt I had to. It was true spiritual empowerment. I was no longer depressed by the idea that success was a faraway goal I had little hope of achieving. Instead, it became something that was now within my reach because there was no pressure on me to reach it.

There is no pressure on you either to reach success. When you let go of the pressure to succeed, you will soon find that success takes on a whole new meaning for you. When you do, you too will enjoy the spiritual empowerment that inspires you to be successful in ways that work for you. You will be able to say to yourself, "Success on my terms!" And that declaration will create a very powerful shift for you.

Declaring you are ready to welcome success the way you want is powerful because you have made a sacred promise to yourself that will awaken you to your real and untapped potential. You can shift from making *something* of your life to making *more* of your life. What exactly that means for you will be revealed during the exciting journey of self-discovery that lies ahead of you.

You and Your Field

I like to compare life to a field. Your field is a field among other people's fields, and all the fields together make up a varied landscape. Each field in this extraordinary landscape, including yours, reflects the beauty of the Universal God Source in its own unique way.

When you first start life, your field is bare, and it's a success. It's enough just the way it is in all its bareness. Your bare field is beautiful and has value. It represents steadfast purity. It is an integral part of nature, *but* it also has potential. It can be cultivated. It can produce wonderful crops. The decision whether to enjoy the bareness of your field or to seed it with your ambitions and dreams is yours.

A bare field is beautiful, and so is a field full of color, energy, and growth. Taking your field (your life) to a different level has now become an invitation and not an order. It has become a matter of personal choice and not a demand. Only you can choose whether to leave your field bare or to cultivate it. If you decide to cultivate your field, you are entering into a truly grand, exciting, and life-altering project.

You may be familiar with the term *self-realization*. Self-realization is one of those concepts that are all the rage these days, especially in the wake of the commercialization of spirituality. Many spiritual teachers are encouraging self-realization and using the term at every opportunity. But what does it really mean to *realize yourself*? And how does one do it?

When I studied the meaning of self-realization, I soon found there are many definitions for this concept. The explanations with which I personally resonate the most stem from Eastern traditions and certain psychologists such as Maslow. Eastern traditions usually define self-realization as the process of awakening to one's own identity and to a connection to a Higher Power. Maslow refers to it as psychological maturation and the development and honing of one's innate skills, gifts, and potential.

I interpret self-realization as a combination of both these definitions. During your personal and spiritual development, I believe you go through a series of awakening moments that inspire and empower you to take action and use your talents in the best possible ways. Self-realization means fully appreciating and then utilizing the grand potential of your field. It is about accepting the invitation your field presents to you to take your life to new heights. Self-realization is about using your current lifetime to soar higher, shine brighter, and feel more fulfilled.

Incarnating on this planet is a big enough feat—a success—but you can maximize your lifetime by using your life as your unique fertile field to plant, cultivate, and harvest your dreams and ambitions. In other words, you can use it to make more of your life—to turn an ordinary life into the life of a lifetime. That is the opportunity—the opportunity of your lifetime.

That opportunity presents itself to you every moment of every day. Your field is always ready and waiting—waiting for you to explore what you can do with it, how you can make it come to life. Your field is the catalyst for greatness to come into your life. It is the extraordinary, divine, and inexhaustible catalyst for turning your life into the life of a lifetime. Are you getting excited about the potential of your field?

Finding the Way to Your Field

Part of the excitement about your field will include finding the way to your field. This pathway can appear to be hidden at times. Just like weeds and rocks can make walking on a footpath treacherous, your field might be overgrown with the weeds of frustration, obligation, disappointment, fear, and self-doubt. It might be filled with the rocks of life's hardships and adversities.

And so you find it more and more difficult to walk in your field. Sometimes you are so inundated with expectations and under such pressure to succeed that you have little choice but to ignore yourself. Again. Self-denial settles over you like a thick heavy fog over your field, restricting your view, disorienting you, and making you feel so powerless that you lose your way. Don't despair. Fog can clear, weeds and rocks can be removed, and the pathway to your field can reveal itself to you. Throughout what follows, I will encourage and support you in finding your field.

However, first I would like you to answer the following questions:

What does your employer want from you? What do your children require from you? What do your in-laws expect from you?
How do your friends like you to behave?
How much time do you spend looking after other people?
How many responsibilities do you have on a daily basis?
Why do you spend so little time on yourself?
Why is it hard for you to say no?
Why haven't you been able to follow through on your plans?

Sometimes it feels like everyone wants a piece of you. You are under constant pressure to report to people in one fashion or another. You feel like you have to explain yourself, that you are accountable, that you somehow owe the world. Your employer, colleagues, and clients are relying on you. Your family, friends, and neighbors all depend on you. And so many other people and events require your energy and support.

You are constantly spreading yourself thin as you try to meet all the demands and expectations. It feels as if your life has already been carved out, and you weren't the one who did the carving. It's as if you were forced into a specific position you didn't choose that comes with a never-ending list of assignments you don't want to do.

Now I would like to ask you another question.

What do you want from your life?

Let me ask you that again.

*What do **you** want from your life?*

Notice the emphasis on you. Everybody else seems to be very good at telling you what you should be doing. But what do *you* think you would like to do with your life?

I want you to reflect very carefully on this question. Please take your time. Think beyond those values and goals society has set as benchmarks, such as becoming wealthy or climbing the career ladder or owning a villa by the beach. Sure, those things can be nice. Being promoted at work can be a great thing. Living comfortably can be terrific. I'm not going to disagree with you when you say money can be a big help in life. It absolutely can. But there's more to life than what money can buy. What is the "more" that you want from your life?

Many of my coaching clients hold very high corporate positions and are blessed with an abundant lifestyle, yet they turn to me for help with addressing a certain lack in their lives. Something is missing. That doesn't mean they've climbed the wrong career ladder. They enjoy their career. But they have also become aware of a need for more, a need for something different. They are restless and unfulfilled. They have recognized a void, and now they want to fill it. However, this time they want to fill it in a very different way. They want to fill it in a way that will give more meaning and purpose to their life. For good.

When a corporate executive realizes there is more to life than a career, this is an awakening. When anyone realizes there is more to their life than what they are currently experiencing, this is an awakening. And I'm seeing these awakenings happening for many people. They are becoming aware of the lack of purpose in their life and of their desire to fill the void with something uniquely meaningful to them.

This is a huge shift in awareness that's taking place, and it is beautiful to witness. It fills me with joy because I know people are opening up to their awakenings, and it won't be long before their lives take significant turns. They are about to embark on whole new journeys of self-discovery and self-illumination that will be so powerful they will alter their lives forever. They are each ready to embark upon a journey with an awe-inspiring destination—their heart.

You too can take this journey. You too can awaken to the fullness of your life. You too can discover the wealth of wisdom your heart has for you. I will take you on this journey. What do you need for the trip? A strong desire to learn and grow spiritually, a willingness to venture beyond the known and into a new level of consciousness, and an openness to being amazed as you discover such priceless treasures as clarity, direction, and fulfillment.

I'm going to help you embark upon this journey the same way I help my coaching clients. I'm going to ask you that last question again, but this time I encourage you to listen on a different level. As you reflect on the question and think about your answer, please listen carefully to the *voice of your heart.*

What do you want from your life?

Can you define what you want? What are your dreams and wishes? Have you ever wondered what your life is really about and what you could do with it? What would change the quality of your life and give more meaning and purpose to it?

You may not receive a clear answer from your heart straight away. Please rest assured that's normal. Heck, you may not know what the voice of your heart is even supposed to sound like! Don't be discouraged. Don't be disappointed if you don't receive crystal-clear guidance at this particular moment. That will change.

It is perfectly okay to feel a void in your life but not be able to hear what your heart tells you about how to fill it. The reason for this is simple. You can't hear your heart because you have been taught not to listen to it, not to allow it to interfere with your life. You have been taught to ignore your heart and to think rationally rather than emotionally. Your upbringing and social conditioning over the years have silenced your heart's voice.

If you don't hear that special voice just yet, it may be because your heart is only whispering right now. The good news is you can give your heart permission to speak louder. It needs your permission to send you clearer signals to help you awaken to your full potential. You grant this permission simply by being willing to *listen.* Your willingness to listen more closely to your heart along with your appreciation for the wisdom it radiates are two of the most important tools you have on your journey of self-realization.

I have great admiration for your heart. It possesses a wealth of wisdom because it plays such a pivotal role in your awakening process. Your heart is the gateway to your soul. In fact, your heart and soul work in tandem.

The soul can channel its dreams and aspirations to you through your heart. Your heart is the passage through which your soul sends you insight about the karmic dreams it holds for its divine evolution.

Does this give you a fresh perspective on the importance of your heart? Now let me tell you how to make the most of this most valuable resource. It's easier than you think! It's true that, without help from the heart, you would probably find listening to the direct call from your soul difficult at best.

Doing so would require a great deal of trust in your ability to "channel" your higher self directly—an ability most of us don't possess, especially in the beginning of our journey.

Channeling your higher self means allowing spiritual guidance to come through without using the emotional guidance system provided by your heart. Direct spiritual guidance from the soul can be perceived by those who have what is called claircognizance. This means they are able to receive knowledge about karmic dreams directly from their higher self by means of thought forms instead of via their heart. This ability can be acquired but usually takes sustained dedication, self-discipline, and learning.

However, receiving guidance from your higher self is not some kind of sacred privilege reserved for the select few. Everybody can tap into their higher self. In fact, we do so far more often than we realize. For example, when we participate in an internal dialogue, we are really tapping into our higher self. I always encourage people who want to tap into their higher self to do it the easy way. I tell them to set aside some time to listen to their heart because it is a lot easier to listen to the heart than to the direct call from the soul.

Your heart works with emotions, and emotions are easier to acknowledge and analyze. Therefore, your heart is an invaluable source of wisdom you want to treasure. From your heart flow your emotions, and from your emotions flow opportunities to become more self-aware. The more you are willing to listen to your heart, the more it will open and speak. And the more you will be able to invoke its wisdom, guidance, and strength.

The ways your heart will infuse you with the grace of its wisdom and guidance can be truly wondrous and at times deeply humbling. Occasionally this wisdom is translated into a very strong emotion, of which you'll suddenly become aware. This emotion that is sometimes so strong it is impossible to ignore is the catalyst that prompts you to take significant action. That's exactly what happened to me a few years ago.

It was a Wednesday evening in March when I rang up my 93-year-old grandfather to say hello. We had a very close bond, and he had always been an incredible source of strength for me. Usually I called him on the weekend, but this time I called during the week.

I said, "Hi, Granddad, it's me, how are you doing?"

To my surprise, he answered, "Chris, I am really, really ready to go."

Usually my grandfather asked me about my life in the UK (he lived in Belgium), and he was always interested to hear how I was doing. But this time was different. He got straight to the point, as if he had been waiting for me to call him so he could tell me he was ready to say goodbye to his current lifetime.

From my heart came an overwhelming wave of compassion and empathy that inspired me to say what my rational mind would never have imagined saying to my grandfather. My heart stirred me to say, "It's okay, Granddad. You are entitled to feel this way. You are allowed to go if you feel ready to do so." I continued, "But I'm jumping on a plane because I want to see you before you go. I will be there on Friday."

Only my heart would prompt me to tell the grandfather I adored that it was okay to die. In hindsight I am fully aware of and eternally grateful for the emotional guidance my heart sent me that evening.

Of course I flew to Belgium and spent a beautiful couple of days with Granddad. The evening I left for the UK, he hugged me in an extra special way. In fact, after I had said goodbye, as I was walking down the hallway of the elderly home where my grandfather lived, he shouted for me to come back so he could give me a second hug. I will always remember that moment. 3 days later, my mother called to tell me Granddad had passed away.

What Is Your Message?

As you awaken to the emotional guidance from your soul via your heart, you will likely become aware of a strong desire to share something with the world, to make a real difference, to leave some kind of mark. If you are feeling that way, then I want to ask you another question to continue your discovery of your life field's potential.

What is your message? What is it you want to share with the world?

Reflect on this question carefully. Your answer contains the seeds of what can become the beautiful and fruitful crops of your field of life. Your message can be large or small. It doesn't matter. What matters is that you know there is value in your message and what you have to share with the world. Tremendous value.

Asking yourself about your message is very powerful—powerful because it is a shortcut to discovering how to fill the void in your life. Doing a little self-enquiry to discover what you really want the world to know can reveal what is needed to bring more purpose and meaning to your life. The better you can define what your message is, the sooner you'll be on your way to adding significantly more personal and spiritual value to your life. Indeed, you will find yourself fully utilizing the opportunity of your lifetime!

People often come to me because they are eager to discover their life purpose. They have tried absolutely everything. They have looked around, tried different career options, and even completed psychometric tests. They are at the brink of giving up on finding that one thing that will give deep satisfaction to their lives. And so they come to me.

When we sit down, they probably expect me to ask them the usual questions. "What are you good at? What do you like doing?" And certainly their answers to those questions can help them come up with some pretty good indications of the direction in which they would like to go. However, in my experience, those questions and answers simply aren't enough—not for my coaching clients and not for me.

So, rather than following the same old, same old path that keeps my clients' life purposes in obscurity, I ask them, "What do you feel your message is? I know you can tell me what you enjoy doing and what you are passionate about, but what is your message? How can you push your inner passion outward to make it relevant for both yourself and the world? What do you want the world to know about that which you are passionate about? Whatever it might be that you're interested in or good at, how can you inspire others through it? How can you help? How will others benefit? How is your passion going to make a difference in people's lives?"

When I ask my clients what their message is, not only do they find it easy to formulate it, but they also seem to receive what I call an "instant download" of information straight from the heart on how their message can play an important role in developing a purposeful way of life. Once people can articulate their message, the doors of their heart swing open and allow further information to come forward. This additional information is worth its weight in gold because it often provides very practical guidance in the form of fresh ideas and inspiration. Suddenly, their life purpose moves from obscurity into clarity, and we are soon discussing the next steps of their journey to make this purpose a practical reality. Tina was a client who worked as a holistic therapist specializing in massage therapy. She was also quite passionate about women entrepreneurship, a passion that was evidenced by the fact she regularly attended business development seminars and networking events on her days off. Despite a challenging economic climate, in less than 2 years Tina had managed to build a successful holistic business from home on a relatively small budget.

During a coaching session, we were talking about her passion for women entrepreneurship. Tina said to me, "I have learned so much about running a successful holistic business these past few months. I have applied many techniques in my own practice with great results. What a shame so many holistic therapists are struggling to find clients." Tina was aware that many of her colleagues, who were often also her friends, were barely able to keep their businesses going.

"Imagine you could address a large group of struggling holistic therapists," I said to Tina, "What would you tell them?"

Tina looked surprised at my question.

"Seriously, knowing what you know about women entrepreneurial skills, what would you tell these therapists? What would your message be?"

Tina didn't have to think twice. "I would tell them that being successful in the holistic business is possible!" She continued with great confidence, "It's possible for everybody as long as you know how. When I think about it, I'm even more passionate about showing my colleagues how to be successful than I am about creating success for myself in my own business."

"Well then, why don't you do it?" I replied. "Why don't you show them how they can achieve what you have achieved?"

"My goodness!" Tina shouted. "You're right! I should! I want to! I could start with a small seminar of my own and share everything I know that can help other therapists succeed. If that works, then I can organize these workshops more often."

102 LIFE OF A LIFETIME

Tina went on excitedly, "My heart glows! This is so exciting! I get to combine my interest in holistic well-being with my passion for women entrepreneurship. And I get to inspire others. This is wonderful!"

Today Tina focuses solely on helping other holistic therapists succeed in business. By defining her message and subsequently listening to her heart's wisdom, she truly has been able to turn her message and passion into a rewarding, purposeful, and meaningful way of life.

I want to make a comparison to everyday life I'm sure you can relate to. It will help you better understand the value of your message. Let's say there's a party tonight and you are standing in front of your wardrobe, trying to decide what to wear. You need to make a choice. Every outfit in the wardrobe is great, and you like all of them. However, you can choose only one. Rather than trying to decide which outfit will make you look your best, ask yourself, "How do I want to come across?" (In other words, what is the message you want to send?)

When you answer the question, "How do I want to come across," you will be able to select the outfit that will complement how you are feeling that night. You will look your best in that outfit because the energy of the outfit matches your own energy. The outfit enhances your appearance in a natural, unforced way.

When you're feeling flat, have you ever noticed how nothing you wear really makes you feel good? People can see right through you. There's no fooling them or yourself. Perhaps you even bought yourself an expensive new outfit to make yourself feel better, but there's something false about it, and your friends pick up on it. They simply know the expensive outfit isn't "you." On the other hand, when you feel confident and happy, you can walk around in any old thing, and everybody will still notice your genuine happiness.

So, my bottom line is, rather than wasting precious time choosing the right outfit (or debating on the right course of action or wondering what your life purpose is), ask yourself what your message is. What do you want to portray? What are you trying to tell the world?

Once you are clear on that, choosing the right outfit (the way forward) will be much easier. When you know how you want to feel (confident, serene, etc.), then you can choose your outfit accordingly. In the same way, if you know the result or impact you want to create, you'll have a better outlook on what steps to take.

Answer the following questions.

What is your message all about?
What do you want people to know?
How can you make a difference in the world?

What to Do With Your Message

Finding your message is one thing. Doing something with it is quite another. Applying your message with diligence is what you're being invited to do in this lifetime. Applying your message is the tool with which to cultivate your bare field so it realizes its potential and turns into a field full of life.

I had a coaching client who did just that. She discovered her message, and now she lives that message. She brought it to life. Let me share her story with you.

Marianne was a successful 38-year-old veterinarian who had always felt there was more to animal care than conventional treatment. Her career in animal health care was going very well, but she felt something was missing. More and more, she found herself opposing the use of conventional medications on pets. She felt very strongly that there had to be a different way, a better way. The call of her heart was to explore what this meant, and she decided to heed her heart's call.

What was the result of listening to that call? Against all advice and criticism from veterinary organizations of which she was a member, Marianne completed further studies and is now a licensed homeopathic veterinarian. Her core message to the world? That there is a drug-free method for helping pets. When I last met with Marianne, she told me her veterinary practice had grown even larger, and her homeopathic treatments attract pet owners from far and wide. I just love how the value of Marianne's message creates real value for her clients, both animal and human!

Nikki's story is another striking example of self-realization. Nikki is a wonderful friend of mine who lives in Belgium and is a nursery school teacher. She is absolutely amazing with young children, and she adores her job. However, some time ago Nikki became aware of a feeling inside telling her to explore further her deep love for working with kids. She longed to do more than her regular work. Her soul and heart were working in tandem, radiating an invitation to explore new ways of educating toddlers other than the traditional methods.

Nikki honored her inner feeling and discovered her message. Her message was about giving children at the youngest age possible an alternative way to explore themselves. She was soon inspired to organize her first Saturday workshop for kids. Nikki didn't organize the typical games where there's a winner and a loser. Instead, she offered the kids creative and fun ways to explore themselves, learn social skills, and express themselves. Those ways included various activities that encouraged group participation such as storytelling, song and dance, working together on a big mural painting, etc.—all ways to create win–win outcomes for all involved.

Nikki's workshops have become very popular, and I am proud of her. The way she has expanded on her skills and gifts is an example of what self-realization is all about. First she listened to her heart, then she became aware of her message, and then she did something with that message. She took it further by looking for ways to expand on her already terrific educational skills. And now those ways bring tremendous enjoyment and value to her own life as well as to the lives of the children and parents who attend her workshops.

Marianne's and Nikki's stories testify to the power of knowing and honoring your message. Both women have worked hard to turn their messages into practical realities. This required dedication and persistence on their part, and the road wasn't always smooth. But they made it. They are cultivating their life fields. And that's what matters to them. They are maximizing the opportunities of their lifetimes, each in her own unique way.

I've said it before, but it bears repeating. Your message can be large or small. It doesn't have to be a message for the big wide world. It can be a message for yourself. Your heart holds many wonderful messages for you, not all of which are meant to reveal your purpose in life. How about simply using your heart's messages to create more daily joy in your life? What would you like to say to yourself? What is it you need to know? What's your heart's desire? What does your heart want you to act upon?

Let's say you have recently felt like you want to take singing classes because you know you have a talent. Perhaps you want to explore this emotional signal and look into singing classes. It's a gentle whisper from your soul delivered by your heart to inspire you. This doesn't mean you need to become the next Maria Callas or Placido Domingo. It is simply a message from your heart inviting you to develop your dormant singing skills. And when you decide to listen to that message and act upon it, you are realizing yourself. You are growing one of the crops in your field. You are allowing yourself to be *more* of who you are.

Inflating a Stubborn Balloon

The other day I saw someone really struggling to inflate a balloon. He eventually succeeded, and the balloon was bright and colorful. Watching this scene, I was reminded how realizing your dreams can feel like trying to inflate a stubborn balloon. Sometimes you need to twist and stretch it and blow really hard until your face turns red. However, once you blow hard enough and you get the right flow of air, you can inflate the balloon more easily. Never stop giving the breath of life to your dreams, even if your face turns red once in a while. If you want to pursue your dreams, just stretch your balloon a bit more, take another deep breath, and find your flow.

You will find your flow when you focus on aligning your outer self with your inner self. The outer self has learned to conform to the expectations of the outside world in which you live. The inner self understands your dreams and talents and true ambitions clearly. When you align the two, it creates the authenticity required to start the process of turning your dreams into a reality. This alignment between the inner and outer selves is one of the great concepts of practical spirituality.

You are authentic and truthful with yourself when your outer self acts upon the guidance from your inner self. Living your truth allows you to look at yourself in the mirror and feel good about yourself. Truth gives you strength. Truth breaks the chains of dependency. Truth doesn't push people away from you; it brings them closer because you aren't hiding anything. Instead, you are showing the world the most authentic version of yourself.

How successful do you consider yourself in this area? Would you say your outer self is aligned with your inner self? Are you thinking one thing but practicing another? Believe me, you don't need to go on a spiritual retreat to some far-off country or lose yourself in the great principles of psychology to find out more about your inner and outer selves. If you want to know how well your inner self is aligned with your outer self, simply (but honestly) ask yourself how congruent your daily life activities are with your message.

For example, if you believe in charity, do you adopt a charitable attitude in general? No matter how small your gesture, are you looking to make a difference every day? Or perhaps you dream of owning your own company one day. Do you just dream, or are you taking the necessary steps and looking into what's required to set up your business? The more congruent your daily actions are with your heart's desire, the easier it will be to manifest that desire.

Overnight Success

I believe following your dreams and ambitions is best done by taking small and realistic steps. So often I meet people who want to achieve overnight success. They want to make it big in life; they want to fly high. That's admirable, but there's a real danger too—the danger of being disillusioned. Genuine success often takes a long time.

Singer Susan Boyle's "overnight success" after winning *Britain's Got Talent* took 35 years. Yes, the breakthrough happened during her famous first audition for the show when her audition became an instant worldwide smash hit on YouTube. But Susan had been taking part in singing competitions for decades without any major recognition whatsoever. Her overnight success was many years in the making. What I find so inspirational is she didn't give up.

Try not to focus too much on your overnight success. Your greatest tool is your determination to move forward, one day at a time, one challenge at a time. When you do that, I assure you that each opportunity, each challenge will lead you to the success you long for. Your determination is the tool that can part the curtains of adversity, disappointment, and struggle.

But if adversity does get in the way of your plans and you lose sight of your dreams, take some time out for meditation and reflection upon what's happening. Never take setbacks personally, and don't panic. Be gentle with yourself. Please don't waste energy worrying or punishing yourself.

What you can't do today due to unexpected circumstances you can always do tomorrow. Or the day after that.

Meditation, as I have said before, doesn't mean sitting still for hours on end, chanting. The slightest conscious effort to spend some quality time in your own company makes for a valid meditation. And when you are in a state of calmness, take the opportunity to have a good ol' chat with yourself, to take stock and determine where you want to try something different. Remember that everything—disappointments included—is part of the process of self-realization.

I cannot stress enough how important I believe it is to see beyond all the challenges and reflect on the phenomenal opportunity your lifetime offers. There is nothing you *must* do, yet you have every opportunity to do anything. There are no obligations, only invitations. You have the opportunity to lock on to your inner guidance system and use it to uncover your dreams. There's something extraordinary about dreams. They follow you no matter what. They want to be honored. They want to come true.

Believe in yourself. Believe you can do it. Know that who you are and what you have to offer to this world has value. *You* have value. You are worthwhile. If there weren't a role for you to play on this Earth, then quite simply you wouldn't be here. The universal casting would be different, and that casting is exactly the way it is supposed to be because it comes from the Universal God Source. And always remember this—you have been cast to play a starring role.

Surround Yourself With Support

If you were to ask any great artist, athlete, or anyone who has achieved success about how they accomplished it, all of them—without exception—would tell you how important it was for them to surround themselves with a support system. A support system is a team of people and resources ready to guide you, keep you accountable, and coach you.

Look for help in order to make the most of your life. Surrender your pride and ask for this help. You will be amazed just how much extra strength and energy you can obtain from your support system. Every time you feel like giving up and letting go of your dream, every time you feel tired and unmotivated, every time you are discouraged and disheartened, if you have a support system in place, you will find it much easier to stay the course.

Whether it is financial help you need, mentoring, emotional support—no matter what you need, ask for it. Set up a support system for yourself. If you don't know where to go or who to turn to, meditate on it. And remember, you can invoke the Universe and your spirit guides to connect you with the right people and resources. When you give a sign to your spiritual helpers that you are ready to meet people or take advantage of resources, these people and resources will intersect with your life and offer the keys to help you proceed. Be willing to receive help and support, and they will be provided to you. They may come in forms other than what you expect, but they may also come in *better* forms than what you had anticipated. Keep an open mind, be patient, and stay positive.

Strong and Empowered

So basically it all comes down to this—you're going to need to do some work. But trust me—it's exciting work! If you put in the effort, the Universe will meet you more than halfway and will more than match your effort. That's the magic of cocreation. I've seen it happen so many times for my clients, and now it's your turn.

However, the Universe needs to know what your goals are. It wants to know what you're working on. So go back to the drawing board and reflect on your unique message and your authentic dreams. Be clear on the direction you want to move into. There's no need to think about all the details yet, but think carefully about what you want to grow in your field of life.

When you are at that drawing board, meditate regularly so you can get still and hear your heart's voice. Your heart will channel the wisdom of your soul to your conscious mind in ways and through emotions you will understand. With every new day, you will better understand these ways

and emotions. The more you learn to connect to your heart and appreciate the directions coming from your soul, the more you will find yourself
trusting this guidance. You will find yourself becoming stronger and more
empowered. You will be excited to explore the dreams of your soul in their
totality. I guarantee you will become fascinated with turning your field
into a personal and spiritual extravaganza!

Demands from society, family, and work will slowly but surely move
to a different place in your life. That doesn't mean you aren't going to care
anymore or you're going to neglect your other work. But it does mean
you will speak up for yourself and make more time for your goals and
projects. You will create space in your life to allow your self-realization
to unfold.

When you trust the guidance of your heart and honor your message,
that unfolding will happen in ways that are perfect for your own personal
expansion and for your soul's own personal evolution. That's how you
cultivate your field of dreams with passion, dedication, and trust, one day
at a time. That's how you grab the opportunity of your lifetime with both
hands and become more of who you are. That's how you truly make the
most of your time here on our extraordinary planet.

Summary of This Chapter

- Your presence on this planet is the current physical manifestation
  of your soul, and so you are a success from the moment you are
  born.
- The measure of the success of your life is very different for your
  soul than for us humans.
- Make a conscious decision to be kind to yourself by releasing the
  need to be overly self-critical and goal obsessed.
- Self-realization is about using your current lifetime to soar higher,
  shine brighter, and feel more fulfilled.
- You can maximize your lifetime by using your life as your unique
  fertile field to plant, cultivate, and harvest your dreams and
  ambitions.
- Your heart is the passage through which your soul sends you insight
  about the karmic dreams it holds for its divine evolution.

- The better you can define what your message is, the sooner you'll be on your way to adding significantly more personal and spiritual value to your life.
- The more congruent your daily actions are with your heart's desire, the easier it will be to manifest that desire.
- Look for help in order to make the most of your life.

You can maximize your lifetime by using it to realize your dreams and ambitions. That is the opportunity—the opportunity of your lifetime.

CHAPTER 7

Your New Way of Seeing and Soaring

"I can't find 'The One,' and it's killing me! When will I find him?"

Lea asked me this common and rather earthly question. What she didn't expect was my not-so-common and rather spiritual answer.

I replied, "What if you can't find 'The One' because he might not exist? What if you are looking for someone you're not supposed to meet? What a waste of your time and energy that would be, right?"

To say that Lea looked at me flabbergasted is an understatement.

"Before you began your current life, it could be you planned to be with a partner for this lifetime. But what if you didn't? Then you are frantically looking for something you didn't schedule to happen. With over 6 billion people on this planet, why don't you begin enjoying people's company for what it is, rather than focusing all your precious energy on finding a possible Mr. Right?"

This may sound like the last thing Lea wanted to hear, but actually it was precisely what she needed to hear to set herself free. It was a fresh perspective on love and certainly very different from Lea's belief about finding Mr. Right. Until then, Lea had believed there was one special person she was destined to be with. But that belief was keeping her prisoner. To use her own words, it was even "killing" her. She was feeling sad and desperate for love, and she had become a slave to her own belief about the need to find her soul mate.

"Wasn't she discouraged when you told her this?" you may ask. Let me tell you that Lea wasn't disappointed one bit. Quite the opposite was true. She felt a sudden and enormous sense of relief. After all, she understood I hadn't told her she would *never* find Mr. Right. What I had said merely created a change in her perspective. Meeting Mr. Right was still possible for her. But, until that encounter took place, she could focus on herself and the many wonderful spiritual connections in her life instead. By discovering a fresh perspective on a belief that was exhausting her emotionally, Lea was able to quickly release that belief and move on.

Do you have beliefs that hold you back? That exhaust you emotionally? Are your fears stopping you? What spiritual questions make you doubt? Whether you are wondering why you still haven't found your soul mate or if you must forgive someone who's badly hurt you in order to move on, it isn't uncommon to experience moments of great questioning, confusion, fear, or doubt on your journey of personal and spiritual awakening.

Because spiritually inclined people are often sensitive people, we have a tendency to be overly analytical and concerned about being on the right track or taking the right course of action. That's normal, and it's important to honor your sensitivity and not to panic or give up when you have moments of feeling insecure. You want to look at these moments as stepping stones. They are stepping stones into an even more authentic version of you. Moments of insecurity and self-doubt are opportunities to look deeper and open your mind to new perspectives that feel right as you search for clarity, answers, and enlightenment. Keeping calm and focused and patient with yourself are particularly helpful when you go through a period of what I call "spiritual overwhelm."

Spiritual overwhelm can occur when you are exposed to an overload of information and then put too much pressure on yourself to know what's spiritually "correct." This is a very common phenomenon. During coaching sessions, I frequently help people who are dealing with spiritual overwhelm and the fear it can cause. They long to set themselves free and make sense of what they are learning and experiencing on their inner journeys. I applaud this, for when they let go of fear, fear lets go of them.

Are you going through a phase of spiritual overwhelm? Are you confused from time to time about who or what to believe or what to do? Do you experience sleepless nights trying to decipher your life purpose or wondering if you're on track? Maybe you have been searching for answers but became even more confused because you were told too many different opinions.

The abundant supply of commercialized New Age teachings is like an ocean of concepts and ideas that collides with the other ocean of influential religious principles. When you are caught in the current between these two mighty oceans, you can easily feel dragged into the murky depths of too much and often contradicting information. You can become deeply confused about what to believe when all you really long for is enlightenment! The good news is there's a way out. You can swim back to the shore of emotional stability quickly.

As you cultivate your life's field, you will have esoteric questions once in a while. Use these questions as stepping stones leading toward your further spiritual awakening. Set yourself free by finding answers you can resonate with. Find your own sense of fulfillment and adopt beliefs that inspire you. Explore releasing dogmatic religious and spiritual principles and letting go of anything you've been told that makes you fearful.

Be your own spiritual authority figure. Allow yourself to move from confusion and contradiction to clarity. And most of all, *enjoy* this process. Life will always be an ongoing search for answers, so don't rush to find them. Instead, honor your sensitive nature. Enjoy discovering new perspectives and feeling lighter with every new insight that resonates with your heart.

I want to share my answers to a selection of frequently asked spiritual questions from clients and seminar guests. These answers have been carefully distilled from my own years of searching for clarity. With much persistent inquiry as well as great excitement, I have discovered explanations with which I can resonate. They are insights from the field of practical spirituality and also obtained through self-reflection and channeling. They are perspectives that have allowed me to stop living in fear and confusion and to create a life of emotional freedom instead. These understandings have helped me on my own journey and can offer you fresh perspectives for your journey too.

"Do I Have to Forgive to Be a Good Person?"

It depends on the situation. If the person who has done you wrong sincerely asks for your forgiveness, then I suggest you forgive them. I am sure you can use your excellent personal judgment to determine if their request is genuine. If the request is an authentic one, then be willing to forgive so you can both move on.

However, if the situation is of such a grave nature you cannot find it in your heart to forgive a person because it seems almost impossible to do so, then please rest assured you can still be a good person. Some offences are so severe they can require an almost superhuman ability to forgive. Even though you are a part of the Universal God Source, in your human capacity during this lifetime you may find it impossible to forgive. This is perfectly acceptable. You have nothing to worry or feel guilty about. However, I believe time is a powerful healer. Who knows? Perhaps in time you will change your opinion and find a way to forgive.

Sensitive people often want to forgive someone who has caused them significant pain because they believe they have to forgive in order to be a good person. Such people have such a strong desire to be good that they risk becoming too good hearted. They may forgive simply for the sake of forgiving or for fear of being punished in the afterlife.

If you recognize yourself in this situation, rest assured you don't *have* to forgive someone to be a good person. Know that the person who has upset you may not even still be suffering. They may have already moved on. If that's the case, the only person who's suffering is you, and now you need to move on too.

You want to find a way to deal with your need to forgive that originates from your desire to feel better. Here's what you can do. Remember that everything is a play on the stage of life. Undergoing the experience is what it's all about. If you undergo the experience of being hurt and upset, then you have succeeded. You are the winner.

You become stronger when you can acknowledge you have undergone a hurtful experience and that you did so to evolve your soul. That's one way to achieve forgiveness. How? Because forgiveness is no longer the main focus. The evolution of your soul becomes your new focus. Look inside and focus on your achievement—your *spiritual* achievement. When you focus on the fact you came through a situation that added to your spiritual growth, you have moved away from the victim position and subsequently gained strength.

Making peace with a situation in which you were caused pain but your forgiveness wasn't sought is crucial for your emotional and physical well-being. Unresolved anger toward and disappointment in those who have done you wrong can cause illnesses on both emotional and physical levels.

Practical spirituality can prevent this by helping you take a fresh look at forgiveness.

An important part of forgiveness is realizing and accepting that what happened is more about the other person and their soul's path of growth than it is about you. Their action was how they thought it best to behave with the wisdom they had at the time. Of course you were at the receiving end of that situation and in that respect it also became an opportunity for your growth as well.

You can't change other people or always expect apologies, but you can change the way you let others' actions affect you. You may feel pain and disappointment, but don't let a bad situation lead you to think you are not a good person. You *are* a good person. And you are wise and strong too. When you accept any disappointing experience as part of your soul's growth, you add to your wisdom and strength.

"I Have a Feeling I Need to Save or Rescue People"

Sensitive and caring people often have a strong desire to help anyone at any cost. As admirable as that may be, it is important to remember that everyone needs to grow in their own ways and in their own time. Of course you can help those you love when they are going through hard times, but you have to be careful with your own energy levels. If you find that helping people is wearing you out, you have to take a step back and allow yourself to rejuvenate. Don't feel guilty about it. Just remember you won't be of much help if you can barely keep yourself going.

Also, if you always keep someone from hitting the proverbial rock bottom, you rob them of the opportunity to experience that bottom and to pick themselves up and rebuild their life. This can be an incredibly difficult perspective for sensitive and caring people to have. But if you and your unconditional support are standing in the way of the people you want to help and their learning opportunity, you are actually prolonging their pain and challenge.

Here's what you can do instead. Let the people you are worried about know you are there when they need you but that they need to give you permission to get involved. Ask them to give you a sign when they require your help. All they need to know is they can call on you. That's sufficient. You make your help available and, rather than exhausting yourself trying to impose your caring and help on to people, you let them come to you instead. When you try this, you will see that people will come to you for guidance when they are ready. And when that happens, they will have a mindset that will welcome your help much more easily. They will be more coachable and more willing to accept your support and care. They win, and you win too.

A final word before we move on. Be sure to check your motives and intentions very carefully when you feel inspired to help someone. You want to be sure you aren't coming from a place of needing to feel needed or deriving power from playing the role of the helper. Be wary of a relationship that seems to be based on rescuing someone. It can feel quite rewarding to play Sir or Lady Galahad, but the truth is you and the person you are rescuing are caught in an unhealthy pattern of relating to each other that doesn't contribute to either person's spiritual growth.

"How Can I Finally Make This 'Law of Attraction' I Keep Hearing About Work for Me?"

By taking a step back. If you feel the Law of Attraction isn't working for you, reassess how you are applying the concept. The truth is you aren't the only one feeling unsure about all of this. The hype around this spiritual law and the suggestion that you can attract into your life anything you think about have certainly attracted one thing into the lives of many—disillusion. The Law of Attraction is indeed a powerful law of the Universe. However, the way it has been packaged and sold has less to do with helping people create a better life and more with selling a much-desired product instead—namely hope. And hope certainly sells. Everybody needs a boost from time to time. So when people are told they can get what they want by simply sending out their wish to the Universe, of course they'll find that fascinating. And of course they'll be disillusioned because it's not quite as simple as all that.

What you need to understand to make the Law of Attraction work for you is that this law is the underlying power in the process of cocreation.

There's a word in there some people seem to overlook—*creation*. Cocreation indicates that you create *together with* the Universe (Source, your guides, etc.) The Universe isn't going to bring your manifested wishes to you on a silver tray. In other words, it's *you* who needs to put in some effort first. This law is not about "ask and sit back," but about "ask and take *action*."

Lots of action and consistently working hard. That doesn't mean you can't take pleasure from working hard. If your goals are inspiring enough, working hard is downright enjoyable.

When you take action, the real guidance from the Universe will soon take place. When you create and take steps toward achieving your goals, the Universe cocreates with you. You will discover that the Law of Attraction is a spiritual channel through which inspiration, means, and opportunities are delivered to you.

It's important to remember that the help will come to you in many different ways. Too many people look up to the skies, waiting for a pot of gold to drop into their lap. That's not what the Law of Attraction is about. It's about your willingness to experience this power as a sense of grace—a force that drives you forward. Who would you rather support and reward in your life? Someone who begs you for help but doesn't initiate action, or the individual who asks for your guidance and coaching while they are busy taking action? You get the point.

In addition to assuming your creative responsibilities, you also need to understand that invoking the Law of Attraction is all about attitude. Pursue your goals and dreams with a positive attitude. If something doesn't work, try something else. Keep going, and don't give up. If you give up, the cocreative energy that comes back to you is also one of giving up, reinforcing the negative spiral downward.

The same is true with frustration and impatience. Be careful. If you become frustrated, you only attract more frustration. For example, if you ask me, "How can I *finally* make this Law of Attraction work for me?" you radiate an energy of impatience and underlying frustration that will keep sending more frustration your way. But when you approach your goals with a positive attitude instead, meaning you are resolute about finding a way to get where you want to go, the cocreative energy will be positive in return.

What I notice is that people apply the Law of Attraction in the hope it will be a quick fix—a miracle pathway to seeing their wishes coming true immediately. When it doesn't happen, they become disappointed. But there is a reason why it doesn't happen—a reason people may not want to acknowledge even though understanding it could help them. The Law of Attraction is always available. However, it doesn't always work when we command it to work. The law works in tandem with the Universal God Source and, in turn, with your soul. Therefore, the reciprocation you'll receive from the Universe will be considerably more apparent on some occasions than on others. Your soul knows when you are going through a learning phase in which you will be better served by a reduction in the speed and flow of energetic reciprocation. So that's what happens, a kind of gentle applying of the brakes for your own good.

Similarly, when you are in a phase when Universal support and guidance will be beneficial to your learning experience, the speed and flow will be increased, and you will find the Law of Attraction stronger and easier to invoke. This is another perspective that can set you free. It can also encourage you to keep taking action and keep moving forward, rather than putting too much hope in the Law of Attraction as your own personal fairy godmother.

Let me give you a very practical example. All the players who take part in a grand slam tennis tournament are eagerly looking to win the title. Let's say initially there are fifty players, but of course there can be only one winner. Only one person out of all the participants will achieve "the dream." Does that mean the Law of Attraction will work strongly enough only for the one person who will win the tournament? Did all the other players, even those who made it into the semifinals, send their wishes out to the Universe the wrong way? Did the other players not assume their role in the process of cocreation well enough? Of course not.

The Law of Attraction is available to every player during the tournament in the same way it is available to him throughout his entire life. But it is not a matter of wishing strongly enough. As is always the case with spiritual growth, it's about seeing the bigger picture. For all the losing players, the motivation to move forward and try a different approach next time lies in the bigger picture. With a bit of willingness, they can look back and recognize how the Law of Attraction might not have sent them the trophy (yet) but many other worthwhile assets may have come their way—a good trainer, new connections, a sponsor who offers a lucrative deal, exposure on television, etc.

The Law of Attraction was very much in action for everybody during the tournament. However, it is always linked to a person's particular stage of spiritual growth and therefore works with precisely the right intensity to contribute to that growth. In the bigger picture, the Law of Attraction has not failed any player. It has generously supported every individual in precisely the right way.

"I Am Interested in Spirituality, but I Am Scared of Death. What Happens to Me When I Die?"

It would be too presumptuous of me to claim I know exactly what will happen when you die. In fact, I believe very few, if any, human beings actually have that information. What I can share with you is what I have come to understand from my own significant research, the paranormal events I've experienced, and the glimpses of the afterlife I've received in the form of visions and channeled information. And, although I'm not in a position to expand on the complexities of the afterlife, I can discuss how you can remove your fears around death.

There is no need to fear death. There is no need to fear *your* death. There is no point in walking through life in fear of what will come after this lifetime. I say this because that which you think of as "after this life-time" merely comes *before* your next lifetime. So the ending is very much a *transition* either into another new beginning if your soul chooses to incarnate again or into your more permanent stay on the Other Side until such time as you return to the God Source. (All souls eventually return to the God Source, but it is a very long-term process.)

Fear of death is a very real fear for many people. For some it is the fear of not managing to do all the things they want to do while they are alive. That's a common fear among people who choose not to believe in an af-terlife. (By the way, belief in an afterlife is not a prerequisite for changing your life or for your personal and spiritual growth.)

However, the majority of people probably believe in some sort of af-terlife but are very confused about it all. I believe it's fair to say this is normal since more questions than answers exist! There is so little known about where you will go, who will judge you, what type of retribution will happen, or whether you'll make it through to what people call "heaven." Much of your fear stems from all those unknowns.

This is why I want to offer my thoughts on what I believe will happen when you reach the end of your lifetime. I deliberately do this in a very simplified way in order to make an incredibly complex concept as straightforward as possible. There is no reason to fear death because there are so many wonderful things to look forward to. No matter how incredibly complicated or unsettled you think your life might be, this will *not* affect your ability to choose between heaven and what I call "not-heaven."

Not-heaven is still the hereafter. Let's be very clear about that. A soul does not cease to exist when a person dies. All souls cross over to another dimension—yes, even the souls of those we believe should never make it to heaven. It isn't up to us to decide. Therefore, let me repeat that *all* souls cross over to another dimension upon physical death. However, there are different types of dimensions, and that is where the differentiation comes into play. That's where your belief will be your compass.

Basically, you can choose to linger in what I call the Dimension of Doubt or celebrate in the Dimension of Clarity. Both dimensions consist of multiple layers (often referred to as levels or spheres). This wide variety in spheres enables souls to choose to take on a capacity ranging from remaining earthbound to becoming a very advanced spiritual being such as a guide.

Even if a soul has been introduced and shown around the Dimension of Clarity, it can willingly choose to go to the Dimension of Doubt because it always has free will. A soul chooses to go to the Dimension of Doubt when it feels it belongs there and never because of punishment.

To get straight to the point, a soul has the opportunity to apply to go to a higher level, but it will choose the level to which it feels most drawn or where it feels most comfortable. The choice of dimension is a reflection of the soul's preference. I have told you before that you are a being of choice and very powerful. It is no different when you arrive in the afterlife.

Of course that means you can also choose to go to the Dimension of Clarity. Again, it will be your choice because your soul will understand precisely in which dimension it can most restore itself. After all, your soul keeps learning in the afterlife. Its journey of growth continues. In both dimensions, you rest your soul, review all of your lifetimes, and determine where you are in the evolution of your soul. Both dimensions are places where you rejoice in the company of those who crossed over to that dimension before you.

What any soul in the afterlife would probably tell you is that the best way to get rid of your fear of death is to focus less on it. I too want to stress the importance of not investing too much time in dwelling on what happens after your life ends. It's what happens *during* your life that counts, wouldn't you agree? Just like our loved ones have done before us, we will all discover what heaven holds for us when we make that journey.

And as with everything in life, that journey will commence when the time is right for your soul.

"Will I Be Punished by God?"

No, you can't be punished by God. Forget about this! You won't be punished because punishment doesn't exist. You can let go of this restrictive and disempowering belief right now. In fact, the invitation to let go of this specific fear is one of the great concepts of spiritual enlightenment. It takes the fear out of spiritual living so you can live a *truly* spiritual and sacred life. Why? Because living in fear is like putting a brake on your personal development. It doesn't serve you or the Universal God Source.

I believe with all my heart that the only way to glorify any Higher Power is to glorify your own Inner Power. You cannot glorify God by living in fear or denying your self-worth. If you are looking to be "chosen," then you must choose yourself. If you are looking to be "saved," then you must save yourself. And just because you choose to do so does *not* mean you aren't glorifying God. Quite the contrary. Glorify God by choosing to focus on your gifts and magnificence rather than your so-called sins and shortcomings. This doesn't mean you will behave in an obnoxious or self-important way. Confidence and enlightenment can radiate from the heart with serenity and be enjoyed quietly. Focus on bringing out your inner strength. There is no punishment—*ever*.

When you make your journey to the hereafter, your soul will review how many self-chosen items on your current life's shopping list you collected in the form of life experiences.

You will not be punished. Instead, you will be blessed with the gift of feedback. This is feedback on how well you have filled in parts of your karma. Karma is the collection of all your shopping lists, and this collection of experiences usually (but not always) spans many lifetimes. As a soul, you will comprehend this feedback. You will recognize where you could have done things differently and also where you excelled. Every experience has value; every experience counts; every experience represents a checkmark in a karmic box.

You can turn your fear of being judged in the afterlife into a motivating and empowering incentive to bring balance back into your life *today.* You can transform your fear into an incentive to do the best you can do *now.* That is the truest, purest, and spiritually most advanced way of releasing your fear of punishment because, when you know you have done the very best you can, your fear will fade and rightfully make way for pride and fulfillment to take its place.

Only you know in which areas of your life you want to make changes. For example, if you are a fiery person and easily feel the need to criticize others, consider making an effort to become calmer around people and notice the positive in them. If you have been missing out on some great opportunities because you are overly analytical or doubtful, then next time take a leap of faith and discover something new.

Your inner state will indicate how well you are doing restoring your balance. The more you find yourself saying, "I feel peaceful inside; I don't need to pretend anymore; I know I'm being who I really am," the more you are getting the balance right. It's that feeling of perfect stillness in your heart and mind when the storm of life rages around you.

Doing what is needed to create that feeling is what authentic personal growth is about. Experiencing that feeling is what authentic happiness is all about. The more you become aware of this feeling, the more confidently you can look forward to receiving your feedback when you complete your journey. It will be much easier to accept your feedback knowing you have made a significant conscious effort to be your best self during this lifetime.

If you are looking for a way to please God or to live a spiritual life, you need to first please yourself and first honor your own spirituality. Let me be very clear. The Universal God Source does not want you to live in fear and uncertainty. The God Source and your soul want you to feel emotionally liberated and able to choose your own beliefs. Please know that no one—neither you nor God—benefits when you choose to live your life in fear, submission, or doubt.

Let this be a spiritual message of strength for you. If you are reading this now, you have likely attracted this spiritual message into your life today because you were ready to spiritually awaken further. Are you ready to increase the flow of encouragement you are experiencing in this very moment? You can do this by releasing any beliefs you have held for years that no longer resonate with you in your heart and soul. In chapter 2, I asked you to write down these beliefs so you could release them later on. That moment has arrived.

What I would like you to do is the following. Take a moment to meditate. Do it now. Close your eyes for the next couple of minutes and relax. I invite you to reflect on the journey you have taken while reading this book. You've learned about your moments of awakening. You've discovered how you are a part of the Universal God Source. You now know you are a powerful soul on an extraordinary mission of growth. You have tools at your disposal to help you boost your self-worth and confidence. Enjoy this moment of calm. Review all you have learned with which you resonate. Isn't it wonderful how much better you understand yourself and your life's journey? Now I want you to carefully read the belief(s) you wrote down in chapter 2. As you do this, listen closely to your inner guidance system. Notice how your heart and soul feel now about what you wrote down back then. Are your old beliefs still giving you that sad feeling of fear and unworthiness? Are those old beliefs still feeling as restrictive as they did back then? Do they still feel programmed, false, and uncomfortable?

I suspect they feel even worse. That's because you have grown so much. You have allowed a major shift in clarity to occur within. You have permitted yourself to become lighter and more spiritually aware. You have opened yourself up to welcoming fresh perspectives on old beliefs that are suppressive and disempowering.

You can now discard those old beliefs altogether or reshape them into beliefs that empower and inspire you. Either choice will greatly enhance your personal and spiritual growth. You, who lives in emotional freedom and knows you are encouraged by the God Source to *enjoy* this freedom, will create space in your heart and mind to welcome new revelations and insights to help you create a truly blessed life.

Summary of This Chapter

- Focus on yourself and the many wonderful spiritual connections in your life instead of exhausting yourself by looking for Mr. or Ms. Right.
- Moments of insecurity and self-doubt are opportunities to look deeper and open your mind to fresh perspectives that feel right to you as you search for clarity, answers, and enlightenment.
- Keeping calm and focused and patient with yourself will be particularly helpful when you go through a period of spiritual overwhelm.
- You don't have to forgive to be a good person. Heal your anger by seeing the hurt you experienced as a learning experience. Forgive when you feel ready to forgive.
- You don't need to save people. Simply make your help available and let people come to you instead.
- The Law of Attraction works in tandem with the Universal God Source and with your soul. Therefore, the reciprocation you'll receive from the Universe will be considerably more apparent on some occasions than others.
- You can turn your fear of being judged in the afterlife into a stimulating and empowering incentive to bring balance back into your life *today*. You can transform your fear into motivation to do the best you can do *now*.
- Don't live in fear and uncertainty. The God Source and your soul want you to feel emotionally liberated and able to choose your own beliefs.

Sometimes we need to dare to soar. For only when we soar higher can we see over the mountains; those mountains were beautiful to look at but have been restricting our view for far too long.

CHAPTER 8

Eight Reasons to Leap Forward

When I was a child, one day I noticed what looked like a postcard that had fallen out of my mother's diary. It was a motivational card with a picture of a frog on it. The frog was sitting on a lily pad drifting in a pond, looking at another lily pad and wondering whether it would be able to leap to the other pad without falling in the water. This was many years ago, and I can still remember the powerful effect the image on the postcard had on me. Even more powerful was the motivational quote written at the bottom of the card—"*Go ahead. You can do it!*"

Now, I wouldn't want to compare you to a frog! But are you sitting there, looking at the next lily pad in your life? Do you want to leap ahead but are contemplating if you should? Do you wonder if it's safe for you to leap? If you will make it? Whether it's the right pad? Or if maybe you should try leaping on another one—maybe one that's a bit closer? I'm about to give you eight good reasons why you *can* leap forward!

Look, even if the frog ends up in the water, it will survive. That's for sure. And so will you. That's also for sure. However, I don't want falling into the water to even be an option for you. You didn't read this book so you could make your leap and fall short. You picked this book because you felt intrigued by what it had to offer. And I believe that means you are ready to bring about some kind of change in your life. Am I right?

That change can be a large project or perhaps a dream you want to realize, such as setting up a business or training to run a marathon. But it can also be a very personal aspiration, such as becoming more confident and self-assured. Or perhaps you want to develop your innate skills and talents further or achieve certain professional goals. *All* types of change are grand in their own unique way. And all types of change are within leaping reach in your pond of life.

When you decide you want to bring about change in your life, you are deciding to embark on a journey. A fascinating journey filled with both hesitation and excitement. A journey to the next phase of your life. Whatever the change you aim for, the journey will lead you to a place where you'll discover many new things and accelerate your personal and spiritual growth. But the only way to discover what the next phase in your life holds for you is to leap toward that next lily pad in your pond. And I want to give you extra motivation to do so. Here's why I believe you can leap forward. Here are the reasons why I say to you, *"Leap ahead! You can do it!"*

Reason 1: You Are Ready

Being ready can be as simple as honoring the feeling of being ready. To be ready doesn't mean you need to have all the resources or the perfect plan. To be ready doesn't mean you need to know what's going to happen and when and how. You don't always need to know what the final result will look like or feel like. That's getting ahead of yourself, which creates unnecessary stress.

It's so easy to say, "I don't think I'm good enough/strong enough/ experienced enough yet." But I want you to stop hiding behind what are often excuses. Your disempowering thoughts create disempowering energy. And because of the contradiction in energies between your desire for change, on the one hand, and your hesitation, on the other, the energetic vibration you send out is one of doubt and confusion. So what do you attract back to you? What do you create more of? Doubt and confusion.

Instead, I encourage you to say to yourself, "I am ready to take my life to the next level. I am ready to move forward in my life." This is a great way to kick-start the process. Use affirmative words that will help you send out a clear and pure energy signal to the Universe. Stating to yourself and the Universe that you are ready will help you feel empowered to take action.

You don't need more diplomas, skills, qualifications, or credentials to take the first step. You can always obtain additional training and acquire the necessary resources later, should they be required. For now, it's all about acknowledging that you are *ready*. It's all about no longer pushing back against your desire for change but accepting and embracing it instead. To acknowledge you are truly ready is the most powerful statement you can make. Saying to yourself you are ready for something different and new—whatever project or dream that might be—is the greatest gift you can give to yourself.

Reason 2: You Are Capable

You are capable of moving into the next phase of your life because there's something you don't know. Let me reveal a secret that's been kept from you. You have untapped stores of energy inside you, lying dormant. These energy reserves can be tapped into only by taking action. In other words, as you take steps toward reaching your goal, you will awaken a powerful force that has been waiting for just this moment. This force will drive you forward. Its energy will fuel you with strength, motivation, and encouragement you never imagined possible and never knew you had because you were never told about them—until now.

Only you know if the calling to reach your goal is real. But if it is, and you get goose bumps simply at the thought of accomplishing that goal, then you have to go for it. And when you do—when you take action— this amazing source of previously hidden energy will help you. It will help you be authentic in your actions and propel you forward. Perhaps even more importantly, this power will be there to pull you out of any temporary slumps you might encounter.

I can promise you this because I know this power well. I work with it every day. It guides me through any hesitations and stress I might experience, and it always leads me where I want to go, no matter how large my goal. I always feel capable of charging ahead and exploring new opportunities in my life. And you can feel this way too, if you let the power coming from your untapped inner energy stores guide you. You'll see!

Reason 3: You Are Loved

Nothing is more powerful than love. When we feel loved and appreciated, we catapult ourselves through life. Nothing is too much, too hard, or too complicated. Nothing scares us, and nothing is out of our reach. We feel we can take on the world and are braver than we've ever been before. Well then, would it not make sense to use the power of love to propel you forward in your life? I think so! No matter how alone, lost, or insecure you might feel, I can assure you that you are *loved*. And you can use that love for the purpose of creating a better life for yourself.

Maybe you are wondering where this love will come from. Well, there is an infinite supply of love available to you, but it comes from a different source, a different realm. This exceptional kind of love is provided to you by your soul and a whole collection of entities such as spirit guides and loved ones who have passed over. They always support you in accomplishing your dreams and goals and offer you unconditional love. I want you to use this knowledge to feel invincible. Every time you have even the slightest doubt or hesitation, visualize your spiritual support system encouraging you and cheering you on. They really do think the world of you, even though they reside in a different world than yours.

Reason 4: You Might as Well

"If you don't try, you'll never know—so you might as well." That's a favorite saying of mine. I use it a lot. It's my to-the-point reply when someone is hesitant about taking steps toward a new opportunity and asks me, "Should I do it?"

I can't predict the outcome, but I know one thing for sure. The only way to find what the future holds is to walk toward it. And the only way to find out what *your* future holds is to walk toward it. So you might as well try.

This isn't even about cocreation or to what degree your life is predestined. This is about simple logic. And often a little logic is the wake-up call you need to see the forest for the trees. Think about this for a moment. How can you know how great the next phase of your life is if you don't try to find out? If you want to leap onto a new lily pad of opportunity in your life's pond, you can't keep worrying about falling into the water. Just like the frog, you are agile and will survive.

Remember, your current lifetime is your chance to be bold, to be different, and to boost your soul—so you might as well. Consider how unique and precious your lifetime is. You might as well do something new and exciting once in a while to make sure you take full advantage of that opportunity. Next time you think to yourself, "Should I do it? Should I try?" I want you to answer with confidence, "Hey, I might as well!"

Reason 5: You Have Permission

One of the biggest reasons why people hold back on following their dreams is that they believe they don't have permission to pursue them. They think positive change is a privilege for others, but not for them. Fragile hopes of becoming a more confident person or working toward achieving a dream are often buried under the crushing self-limiting belief that they are not allowed to create a better life. Some people choose not to believe they are as entitled to positive change as the next person.

I am going to make a request. I want you to take a good deep look inside and ask yourself an incredibly important question. Can it be that one of the reasons why you haven't taken any steps toward changing your situation is that somehow you believe you don't have permission to do so? Have you been holding back from jumping at great opportunities because you thought you weren't allowed? That for some reason it wasn't appropriate for you to do so? Do you have a voice in your head whispering (or shouting), "Who the heck do you think you are?"

Don't feel typecast by the societal role you have taken on thus far or by descriptive labels people have assigned you that don't apply. Let's say you were told you were shy as a young child. You believe this and, as a result, you often feel shy. Therefore, people start to perceive you as that shy person. And so you translate your shyness (which you never really had but took on because you were told you were shy) into a belief you are weak and will always remain in the shadow of others. You think there's no place for you in the limelight. Your shyness has taken root, and you now feel totally stuck on the sidelines.

However, just because you feel you can't go anywhere that doesn't mean there's nowhere to go. You can cut yourself loose. You can become a stronger and more self-assured person. You can because you are *allowed* to. You have the permission to change or cast off a description that never applied to you to begin with. No matter what the external or internal pressure, you have every right to try something new. You have permission to change your mind about who you think you are and what you think you are capable of doing. You are allowed to change yourself.

Reason 6: You Will Learn

Everybody is nosy. Whether we admit it or not, we all like to know what's going on, right? We have a curious side and like to be kept in the loop. I believe that's a good thing as long as we don't waste our time on speculating and gossiping. Are you nosy? Good. Do you know what that tells you? It indicates you are eager to learn. You want to learn about everything that goes on in the world around you.

Did you know you can use your curiosity to move to the next stage of your life? Absolutely! It's a spiritual two-for-one. You get to learn *and* you get to move on! You can use your eagerness to learn new things to help you achieve your goals. Just imagine how much will be revealed to you over the next coming weeks or months if you start taking action today. Think for a moment just how much you will have learned by this time next year. Fascinating things about yourself, your hidden potential, your possibilities, the new people you will meet along the way, the new ideas to which you'll be exposed—the list is endless. All waiting for you to discover!

Be an adventurous pirate on your ship of personal growth sailing the sea of change. Look at every challenge, project, or goal as your own personal treasure hunt. Use your desire to quench your thirst for knowledge as your incentive to take action. When you take action, you are bound to discover and unlock the treasure chest that contains wisdom you will be glad to receive. You will be equally glad you didn't waste any time and embarked on your journey *today*.

Reason 7: You're Going to Love It

My clients come from many different cultures and walks of life, and they want to talk to me about a wide variety of issues. But no matter how different their personalities and goals may be, they all experience the same thing shortly after they begin taking action and making changes. They all experience what I call *the joy of achieving*.

This joy is a deep and genuine feeling of happiness, a sense of real satisfaction and fulfilment. This joy is the best of the best of feelings. Some people want to shout it from the rooftops; others prefer to bask in their happiness in a quieter way. No matter how you choose to express the joy of achieving, you can't help but radiate happiness. This is what it feels like when you follow your dreams. It's a reward of the highest preciousness. This kind of joy is unique. It will fill you with the greatest sense of achievement, and you will feel you've made a giant leap forward in your life.

You will love this incredible feeling, and I want you to keep this feeling in mind while you are working on your goals. It's certainly another major reason to go for it and start taking action today. Just imagine how absolutely awesome you will feel when you achieve your dreams! And the good thing is you will already begin discovering the joy of achieving *during* the process. As you jump over the inevitable hurdles you'll encounter, each time you make a successful jump, you will discover just how great achieving feels.

Even in its most modest portions, this joy will become a positive addiction, and you'll want more of it! All those little bits of joy will add up, and when you complete your project or achieve your goal, the grand total will be a massive feeling of authentic inner joy. This joy will be unlike anything you've ever experienced. You will simply adore it. And rightly so, because it will be the well-deserved reward for your commitment and dedication to pursue your dreams.

Reason 8: You Will Become a Beacon of Light

Have you ever gone for a walk by the water and marveled at a beautiful swan? This proud and majestic creature glides through the water effortlessly. Or at least that's how it seems. What we often forget is that, beneath the surface, the swan is paddling like crazy. Without this effort, she would merely drift with the current rather than move toward her destination.

The swan is a symbol of *transformation* as she changes from an unremarkable-looking little gray cygnet to a magnificent white swan. She symbolizes the transformation from small and fragile to strong and proud. And transformation is what this book is about. You have been given the tools to change yourself and your life. But your transformation requires some paddling from you. You too can glide through life, but you will need to put in some effort and use the tools.

Now, as you make this effort and gradually change your life to one of joy, another amazing thing happens. Aside from creating a better life for yourself, there is an additional benefit to look forward to throughout your personal transformation. You will inspire others. As you become stronger, you will become a beacon of light for others. As you discover the joy of achieving, others will notice how you radiate contentment and happiness.

Similarly to the steadfast effort and the motion of the swan creating ripples on the water, your genuine happiness, success, and renewed appreciation for life will also create ripples. Your positive attitude and actions will inspire others to follow your example. Your energy and enthusiasm will encourage others to create their own ripples, their own waves. As you incorporate the tips and techniques from this book into your everyday life and as you further develop your interest in practical spirituality, your inner light is going to shine more and more. The more happiness you radiate, the more people will notice your light. And as you continue your journey, you will discover new ways of shining your light brighter and brighter, and more and more people who are ready for a better life will be drawn to it.

Being a beacon of light is easy; it doesn't require any effort at all. You can inspire by example, simply by being your beautiful and authentic self. Show the world how happy you are becoming. Show others what it feels like to glow and grow. As you do this, whether you are aware of it or not, you create moments of awakening for other people. And just like your own moments of awakening formed the foundation of your transformation, other people will have their own moments of awakening that will inspire them to discover their authentic happiness through understanding their life and their journey. When you inspire by example and lead the way for others while discovering the splendor of your own path, you help others build their own lives of a lifetime. Think for a moment what a gift that is and how it makes your own journey extra special!

Throughout this book I have talked to you about how you are a soul on a journey. You came to this world for a reason. That reason is to participate in as many experiences as you possibly can to contribute to the evolution of your soul. I hope this book has helped you awaken to your own divinity, inner power, and strength. But also to the beauty and the potential of life—the grand opportunity that life is in so very many ways.

Perhaps you now have a clearer idea of what message you want to share with the world. Or maybe you are especially motivated to invite changes into your life. Or perhaps you feel a fresh sensation of confidence and self-empowerment. Whatever the way this book created moments of awakening for you, I sincerely hope you make a commitment to yourself to follow through on those moments. Start implementing today what you have read and resonated with in this book.

I am filled with excitement at the thought of just how much your life can change in so many wondrous ways. I have said it many times before and I want to say it one last time. If I can do it, so can you!

I included these eight reasons to leap forward into the next phase of your life because I wanted to give you an extra boost. Allow these reasons to inspire you to jump at the chance of taking your life to another level. See just how ready, empowered, allowed, supported, and capable you are of flowing into freedom and achieving your goals. And, above all, see how deserving you are of having more fulfilment in your life.

Discover what lies around the corner for you. Discover the joy of achieving. Discover the delight that comes from turning your ordinary life into a life of lifetime!

Index

OTHER TITLES IN THE HUMAN RESOURCE MANAGEMENT AND ORGANIZATIONAL BEHAVIOR COLLECTION

- *The Illusion of Inclusion: Global Inclusion, Unconscious Bias, and the Bottom Line* by Helen Turnbull
- *On All Cylinders: The Entrepreneur's Handbook* by Ron Robinson
- *The Resilience Advantage: Stop Managing Stress and Find Your Resilience* by Richard S. Citrin and Alan Weiss
- *Successful Interviewing: A Talent-Focused Approach to Successful Recruitment and Selection* by Tony Miller
- *HR Analytics and Innovations in Workforce Planning* by Tony Miller
- *Success: Theory and Practice* by Michael Edmondson
- *Leading The Positive Organization: Actions, Tools, and Processes* by Thomas N. Duening, Donald G. Gardner, Dustin Bluhm, Andrew J. Czaplewski, and Thomas Martin Key
- *Performance Leadership* by Karen Moustafa Leonard and Fatma Pakdil
- *The New Leader: Harnessing The Power of Creativity to Produce Change* by Renee Kosiarek
- *Employee LEAPS: Leveraging Engagement by Applying Positive Strategies* by Kevin E. Phillips
- *Feet to the Fire: How to Exemplify and Create the Accountability That Creates Great Companies* by Lorraine A. Moore
- *Deconstructing Management Maxims* by Kevin Wayne
- *The Real Me: Find and Express Your Authentic Self* by Mark Eyre

Announcing the Business Expert Press Digital Library

Concise e-books business students need for classroom and research

This book can also be purchased in an e-book collection by your library as

- *a one-time purchase,*
- *that is owned forever,*
- *allows for simultaneous readers,*
- *has no restrictions on printing, and*
- *can be downloaded as PDFs from within the library community.*

Our digital library collections are a great solution to beat the rising cost of textbooks. E-books can be loaded into their course management systems or onto students' e-book readers. The **Business Expert Press** digital libraries are very affordable, with no obligation to buy in future years. For more information, please visit **www.businessexpertpress.com/librarians.** To set up a trial in the United States, please email **sales@businessexpertpress.com.**

Lightning Source UK Ltd.
Milton Keynes UK
UKHW02f1824150118
316207UK00006B/161/P